BLOODAXE CONTEMPORARY FRENCH POETS

Throughout the twentieth century, France has been a dominant force in the development of European culture. It has made essential contributions and advances not just in literature but in all the arts, from the novel to film and philosophy; in drama (Theatre of the Absurd), art (Cubism and Surrealism) and literary theory (Structuralism and Post-Structuralism). These very different art forms and intellectual modes find a dynamic meeting-point in post-war French poetry.

Some French poets are absorbed by the latest developments in philosophy or psychoanalysis. Others explore relations between poetry and painting, between the written word and the visual image. There are some whose poetry is rooted in Catholicism, and others who have remained faithful to Surrealism, and whose poetry is bound to a life of action or political commitment.

Because it shows contemporary French poetry in a broader context, this new series will appeal both to poetry readers and to anyone with an interest in French culture and intellectual life. The books themselves also provide an imaginative and exciting approach to French poets which makes them ideal study texts for schools, colleges and universities.

Each volume is a single, unabridged collection of poems presented in a parallel-text format, with the French text facing an English verse translation by a distinguished expert or poet-translator. The editor of each book is an authority on the particular writer, and in each case the editor's introduction presents not only a critical appreciation of the work and its place in the author's output but also a comprehensive account of its social, intellectual and cultural background.

The series itself has been planned in such a way that the individual volumes will build up into a stimulating and informative introduction to contemporary French poetry, giving readers both an intimate experience of how French poets think and write, and a working overview of what makes poetry important in France.

BLOODAXE CONTEMPORARY FRENCH POETS

Series Editors: Timothy Mathews & Michael Worton

Timothy Mathews is Professor of French at University College London. His books include *Reading Apollinaire: Theories of Poetic Language* (Manchester University Press, 1987 & 1990) and *Literature, Art and the Pursuit of Decay in 20th Century France* (CUP, 2000). He co-edited *Tradition, Translation, Trauma: The Classic and the Modern* (OUP, 2011) with Jan Parker, and co-translated Luce Irigaray's *Prières quotidiennes/Everyday Prayers* (Larose/University of Nottingham Press, 2004) with Irigaray. The first volume in this series, *On the Motion and Immobility of Douve* by Yves Bonnefoy, has an introduction by him.

Michael Worton was Vice-Provost and Fielden Professor of French Language and Literature at University College London. He has published extensively on contemporary French writers, with two books on Michel Tournier, and co-edited *Intertextuality* (1990), *Textuality and Sexuality* (1993), *Women's Writing in Contemporary France* (2003), *National Healths: Gender, Sexuality and Health in a Cross-Cultural Context* (2004), *Liberating Learning* (2010) and *French Studies in and for the 21st Century* (2011). The second volume in the Bloodaxe Contemporary French Poets series, *The Dawn Breakers* by René Char, is introduced and translated by him.

BLOODAXE CONTEMPORARY FRENCH POETS: 6

PAUL ÉLUARD

Unbroken Poetry II

Poésie ininterrompue II

Translated by
GILBERT BOWEN

Introduction by
JILL LEWIS

BLOODAXE BOOKS

BLOODAXE CONTEMPORARY FRENCH POETS: 6
Paul Éluard: *Unbroken Poetry II*

Original French text of *Poésie ininterrompue II*
by Paul Éluard © Éditions Gallimard 1953.
English translation © Gilbert Bowen 1996.
Introduction © Jill Lewis 1996.

ISBN: 978 1 85224 134 6

This edition published 1996 by
Bloodaxe Books Ltd,
Eastburn,
South Park,
Hexham,
Northumberland NE46 1BS.

www.bloodaxebooks.com
For further information about Bloodaxe titles
please visit our website and join our mailing list
or write to the above address for a catalogue.

Supported using public funding by
**ARTS COUNCIL
ENGLAND**

Bloodaxe Books Ltd, the translators and the series editors
wish to thank the Ministère des Affaires Étrangères, Paris,
and the Service Culturel, the French Embassy, London,
for their assistance and for help given towards translation costs.

Digital reprint of the 1996 edition

CONTENTS

Poésie ininterrompue II

Unbroken Poetry II

GENERAL EDITORS' PREFACE

The Bloodaxe Contemporary French Poets series aims to bring a broad range of post-war French poetry to as wide an English-speaking readership as possible, and it has specific features which are designed to further this aim.

First of all, each volume is devoted to a complete, unabridged work by a poet. This is designed to maintain the coherence of what a poet is trying to achieve in publishing a book of poems. We hope that in this way, the particular sense of a poet working within language will be highlighted. Secondly, each work appears in parallel translation. Finally, each work is prefaced by a substantial essay which gives a critical appreciation of the book of poetry, of its place in its author's work, as well as an account of its social and intellectual context.

In each case, this essay is written by an established critic with a love of French poetry. It aims not only to be informative, but also to respond in a lively and distinctive way to the pleasures and challenges of reading each poet. Similarly, the translators, often poets in their own right, adopt a range of different approaches, and in every case they seek out an English that gives voice to the uniqueness of the French poems.

Each translation in the series is not just faithful to the original, but aims to recreate the poet's voice or its nearest equivalent in another language: each is a translation from French poetry into English poetry. Each essay seeks to make its own statement about how and why we read poetry and think poetry. The work of each poet dovetails with others in the series to produce a living illustration of the importance of poetry in contemporary French culture.

TIMOTHY MATHEWS,
MICHAEL WORTON,
University College London

INTRODUCTION

Of poetry, politics and desire

This volume brings into English the last poems Paul Éluard worked on before his death, at the age of 57, in November 1952. Éluard completed the preparation of the manuscript before the illness leading to his death had become apparent. *Unbroken Poetry II* was published posthumously in 1953.

At a time when still, even in 1996, only a sparse selection of Éluard's poetry is available to the anglophone world, these poems open a poignant door into a prolific poetic output spanning some 35 years. Éluard's work as a poet was framed over these years by a continuing engagement with political contestations of the status quo. His cultural and political trajectory is not tangential but intrinsic to what moved him as a poet and placed his work within his contemporary world. His active involvement with the contesting agendas of Dada and the Surrealist Movement marked his work and his thinking about writing and art for the rest of his life. Active in Surrealist pro-Communism and anti-colonialism of the late 1920s and early 1930s, he also identified with vociferous anti-Stalinist critiques of the parti communiste français (PCF – the French Communist Party) in the mid 1930s. His sense of the world he lived in, and his work as a poet within it, were crucially affected by ascendant anti-fascist responses to events of the Spanish Civil war and advancing Nazism. His active experience of Resistance activities in occupied Paris, and of the PCF's political and cultural centrality in that Resistance, along with the emotional imagery of communist discourse during the Cold War period from the end of the war, strongly influenced his concerns from 1942 until his death.

However, Éluard is taught, anthologised and explicated in France predominantly as one of the greatest love poets of the twentieth century, with emphasis usually on the 'pure', 'radiant', 'innocent', universalising dimensions of his work. His political concerns are frequently seen as occasional addenda, usually on the basis of texts from the Resistance years. His poetry does indeed invoke processes of desire, from his earliest to his final works. He traced the most finely nuanced landscapes of intimacy, and yet also set 'love' in a charged relationship to social conventions and political agendas. Individual poems "about love" are often isolated by critics as exemplary depictions of the universal love celebration we are all supposed to recognise. But, either internally to individual poems or by their juxtaposition with differently angled texts, the poems persistently stand at odds with liberal bourgeois values, conservative sexual conventions and social beliefs. They are written in wider, contestatory dialogue with the violence of militarism and what Éluard saw as the passive indifference, the self-serving and individualistic complicity with injustice and inequalities promoted by capitalist society. They also trace dilemmas of the gendered terrain of heterosexuality, even as they lean into invoking the heterosexual couple as a site of pleasure and liberation. Love poems from all periods of his writing are passionately read in France today by contrasting constituencies of readers – those for whom Éluard embodied the heyday of Surrealist experimentation or the intimately inspired spirit of anti-fascist Resistance; contemporary teenagers, directed by school-text presentation of his work towards the universal, recognisably familiar impulses of emotion which his poetry can be read to evoke; communists, right up until the late 1980s, celebrating in Party-affirming terms the love/politics, Party-member configuration of his poetic output; artists, prolonging the outstanding tradition of poetic-artistic collaboration Éluard sustained; new wave Surrealists, sifting out the most provocative edges of Éluard's images and collaborative texts which speak still now into a transgressive erotic, and provoke disorderings of logic. In the 1970s Éluard could be denounced in moments of sweeping feminist backlash against Surrealist patriarchal sexism or elsewhere claimed by feminist reproductive rights activists using banners showing the plate Picasso had made with the text of the last stanza of 'Le Château des pauvres'/'The Castle of the Poor', which ends this collection.

Éluard's writing triggers emotion in a mostly simple vocabulary that is often charged with unusual combinations of images, with condensations of syntax and displacements of the notion of narrative logic in the poem – key elements of the Surrealist venture itself. A close exploration of the entirety of his poetic production reveals that he wrote poignantly of the desperate quest for the desirable, loving woman who would anchor a masculine subject in a viable sense of reality, a safe relationship both to the world and to himself. He elaborated erotic fantasies moulded by, the cultural traditions of heterosexuality and its language of gender oppositions and with an anxious investment in them. But he charted not only the compulsion to envisage the desired/desiring object in the discursive landscapes of patriarchal cultural traditions, and within conventionally gendered, phallocratic positionings. His agenda also came to evoke and poetically script the problems inherent in that compulsive quest itself. From his earliest writing the dilemma of gender and desire is on stage:

> ...always the same confession, the same youth, the same pure eyes, the same ingenious gesture of her arms around my neck, the same caress, the same revelation. But never the same woman. The cards said I will meet her in my lifetime, *but without recognising her*. In love with love itself.

His love poems celebrate the fantasies, the arrangements and interpretations which the feminine love object is supposed to 'inspire', the celebratory moment of 'the couple', but often only on a quicksand of failure, doubt and uncertainty. Love is a place of loss and perpetual need:

> The sad gentle truth
> That love resembles hunger and thirst
> But is never satiated

Desire underlines the fragility of subjective coherence and the temporary nature of confidence and celebration. The rituals of approaching the desired woman, the poet's culturally authorised and authorising mapping of 'her' in the trajectory of 'his' desire repetitively held Éluard in the tensions of the masculine subject position. At the same time, he saw himself entrenched in a vocabulary and a syntax which sabotaged his own agenda of desire, connection and happiness that his poetic language attempted to capture:

> How do concrete namings invade me
> On this wave of abstractions
> Persistent repetitive
> Drowning me

The quest for a loved, feminine object produced in language activated a set of discursive and political dilemmas which in the end the poetic project could elaborate and trace, but, for Éluard, never complacently or arrogantly resolve. And alongside the project of representing, of endlessly reconstructing and deconstructing these gendered positions, a political discourse informed his reassessments of, and experimentations in, the heterosexual love conventions. In his preface to Valentine Penrose's *Dons des féminines / Gifts from the Feminine* (1951), he mused on the complications of gender he had no illusion of transcending – or of avoiding:

Knowledge of women belongs to woman. To be able to say 'belonged', a whole bizarre, absurd world, that clings tenaciously to the past, virtually adrift from the present, would have to be radically abolished. It lives off memories... I t will perish, and deserves to. I have lived in this impossible world. I suffered from its singular way of life, but I struggled to live and I lived in order to struggle.

Éluard had invested in notions of the enabling power of love even as he depicted its inherent fragility and explored its contradictions. As he worked to re-evaluate love in the light of the uncertainties and problems of gender positions within the narratives of heterosexual desire, he also worked to relate the processes and the high stakes of this dilemma to the political arena of his life. From the mid-thirties, the project of the lovers in Éluard's texts was to be more and more envisaged as a microcosm of a political world of:

couples...
...armoured with daring
Because their eyes face each other
And their goal lies in the lives of others.

Moments of passionate connection, left in earlier texts in their self-contained tunnels of desire and pleasure, were to become frequently qualified by the need to see them also as the beginning of something else, as the initial recognition of different forms of potential enablement premised on the necessity of connection; and as exemplifying the possibility of a larger solidarity. But the voluntarist desire for solidarity, to be emulated from the complex potential of the couple, met political landscapes on the other side of the fence, permeated with another set of dilemmas. Éluard was writing within the evolution of left-wing politics framed by polarisations between capitalist, colonial coalitions and the Stalinisation of Soviet Union communism, each disrupted violently by the invasions of Fascism. Within these contexts, and within the social realities and mirages that were thrown up, he repeatedly turned to investigate the strategic relation of art to questions of social change. Éluard's poetic project moved on territories marked by tensions between deeply political aspirations and the complexity of the maps and languages available. However, his vision of a love text which constructs a desiring self committed to change the world, on the basis of that very love experience itself, developed as central pivot to his poetics and politics from the 1930s onwards. This reaches a powerful climax in *Unbroken Poetry II*.

Dada, Surrealism, communism: the Gala years

Éluard was born in 1895, named Eugène-Émile-Paul Grindel, at St Denis, a provincial town that was expanding but not yet a victim of the sprawling industrial spread that was later to mark it, on the northern outskirts of Paris. The Grindel family thrived there – his father, of peasant origin, as an accountant, and his mother, who had grown up in poverty, as a dressmaker. His father went into the property market, buying and selling land for development, and his mother opened a dressmaking atelier with several employees. In 1908 they moved right into Paris, and began yearly visits to Switzerland. In 1911 Paul took an English language course at Southampton. In summer 1912 he was diagnosed with tuberculosis, and began treatment for an ailment which was to haunt him recurrently. He was the Grindels' only child, and they sent him for a year and a half on a cure at an elite sanatorium in Switzerland. Here began his passionate encounter with his fellow patient Gala (Hélène Dmitrievana Diakonova), a Moscow lawyer's daughter. He read prolifically during his cure, and was already committed to writing. In 1913 his first book of poems, prepared by correspondence, appeared with a small press in Paris.

Back in Paris in February 1914, his *Dialogues des inutiles / Dialogues with Useless Men* was published under the pseudonym of Paul Éluard, the surname being that of his maternal grandmother. When war broke out in August he became an auxiliary conscript and was drafted into the hospital nursing corps, where he worked with victims of trench warfare. In 1916 he requested transfer into an infantry combat unit, but within months was withdrawn from the Front due to ill health. After months of intense correspondence, Gala arrived from Moscow in early 1917 to marry him during one of his leaves. *Le Devoir et l'inquiétude, poèmes suivis de Le Rire d'un autre / Duty and Anxiety, poems followed by The Laughter of Another* came out in 1917. Their daughter Cécile was born in May 1918. *Poèmes pour la Paix / Poems for Peace* appeared four months before the November armistice in 1918.

After the war Éluard worked for his father in property and planning, with his heart and energy, however, leaning towards the post-war literary milieux. Dada had erupted in Switzerland under Tzara's and Ball's influence, and flourished in Spain, Germany and the USA before the end of the war. Éluard read avidly, abreast of new literary currents. In 1919 he met Breton, Aragon and Soupault, from the review *Littérature / Literature*, and began corresponding with Tzara in Zurich. When Dada "hit" Paris in 1920, Éluard founded and edited six issues of a Dadaist paper, *Proverbe / Proverb*, contributed to others – *Cannibale / Cannibal, 391, Bulletin Dada / The Dada Bulletin* – and took part in the strange array of provocative, exhibitionist outings, events and performances Dada staged in Paris. In 1921 he published *Les Nécessités de la vie et Les Conséquences des rêves / The Essentials of Life and The Aftermaths of Dreams*, with an introduction by Jean Paulhan. In 1949 he was to republish together these early poems written between 1913 and 1921. He went to Cologne in 1921 to meet Max Ernst, whose painting intrigued him – a key encounter which had deep creative and emotional influence on Éluard over the next years. After siding with Tzara against Breton in Dada's death-throes, Éluard rejoined Ernst in Cologne. In 1922 they published two extraordinary, disturbing collaborative books juxtaposing Ernst's lithographs with short prose pieces by Éluard – *Répétitions / Repetitions* and *Les Malheurs des immortels / The Grief of Immortal Men*.

After summer 1922 in the Tyrol with Gala, Tzara, Arp and Ernst, Éluard welcomed Ernst to live with him, Gala and Cécile in Paris. The two men met with the Surrealist group which was beginning its experimental sleep séances, working with dreams and hypnosis. The Éluard ménage moved to Eaubonne, to a house whose interior Ernst decorated with a series of fantastic frescoes, which were rediscovered and restored in the 1970s. The three lived in shared sexual intimacy, pitted against the proprietorial monogamy of the bourgeois family. Éluard's work for his father was their main source of income. The complex emotional temperature at home and Éluard's intense dislike of his job reached a crisis for him in 1924. He unexpectedly absconded with funds from his father's business and left on a completely unannounced voyage around the world. He left at the moment of publication of *Mourir de ne pas mourir / Dying of Not Dying*, his first major poetic work, prefaced with a portrait of him by Ernst. Seven months later, forgiven by his father and urged home by his cohabitees, he returned to France. Gala and Ernst sold some of Éluard's art collection to go to meet him to return together from Saigon. Éluard's journey was not to be mentioned again, ever. It hangs like a bizarre event in the pages of Surrealist history.

Éluard returned to be a central member of the Surrealist group and their newly established Bureau of Surrealist Research. Their first tract, *Un cadavre / A Corpse*, responded provocatively to the death of Anatole France. The first Surrealist group manifesto was launched by Breton in November 1924, followed by the first issue of their journal *La Revolution surréaliste / The Surrealist Revolution.* Soon after appeared a concise statement of Surrealist intent, the *Déclaration du 27 janvier 1925 / The January 27th Declaration:*

> We have no interest whatsoever in literature...(Sur)realism is not some new, easier means of expression, nor a kind of poetic metaphysics. It is a means for total liberation of the mind...we are committed to making a revolution.

Here Éluard's name stood with 25 others including Aragon, Artaud, Bosquet, Breton, Crevel, Desnos, Ernst, Leiris, Masson, Naville, Péret, Queneau and Soupault. Éluard and Benjamin Péret published their *152 proverbes mis au goût du jour / 152 Proverbs in contemporary mood* – a list of Surreal rewritings of common-sense formulae.

The Moroccan war broke out in April 1925, and the French colonial army brutally repressed the revolt led by Abd-el-Krim. Éluard endorsed and wrote pieces denouncing French colonialism, racism and the use of military violence to repress national independence struggles. The issue galvanised closer dialogue and collaborations between the Surrealist group and two Marxist, PCF-leaning groups at the journals *Clarté* and *Philosophes. The Surrealist Revolution* and the Communist Party's *L'Humanité* published a joint Communist and Surrealist statement, denouncing the inhumanity at the base of Western civilisation and the 'lies of Europe', calling for opposition to the Moroccan war and for a social revolution at home. A Surrealist denunciation of Claudel placed his work within these problematic terms of French civilisation. Meanwhile Éluard's new collection of poems *Au défaut du silence / In the Absence of Silence* came out in a limited edition, accompanied by twenty of Ernst's drawings, and his poems appeared in the catalogue to a Paris exhibition of Klee's painting.

During 1926 Éluard published four articles in *Clarté* which had close connections with the international communist movement. He wrote here on the revolutionary visions of the Marquis de Sade, Petrus Borel, Lautréamont and Rimbaud. In September, Éditions de la N.R.F. doubled the usual print number of his other works when they brought out Éluard's new collection *Capitale de la douleur / Capital of Pain.* A more modest imprint of another work, headed by a portrait by Max Ernst, *Les Dessous d'une vie ou la pyramide humaine / Undercurrents of a Life or The Human Pyramid,* followed in December. In the meantime, Éluard was one of the five Surrealists who joined the French Communist Party, following debates Pierre Naville had generated within the Surrealist group about the status of Surrealist commitment to revolution and to social political change, and the dilemmas of artistic non-alignment. Breton, Aragon, Péret, Unik and Éluard enrolled in September 1926, and Éluard's name appeared on the collectively drafted texts circulated to explain their decision.

From 1927 Éluard and Gala were spending long periods apart. Éluard's mother had by now assumed the central role in raising Cécile. Gala travelled to Leningrad, Berlin, Switzerland, other parts of France, often acquiring new additions to Éluard's book and art collections. They kept in touch by correspondence and acted out the agreed-on sexual independence they had enshrined at the heart of their relationship. Éluard's letters to Gala (which he asked Gala to promise to destroy, but which she in fact published in 1986) show him painfully fixated on her, with a deployment of erotic fantasy which, more than actually being together, fired the relationship. Éluard and Ernst had a major, but temporary emotional estrangement in 1927, which Éluard interestingly likened to the conflict between Rimbaud and Verlaine. Éluard was often unwell in these years, and his publication of *Défense de savoir / Knowledge Forbidden*, headed by a de Chirico painting, in early 1928, preceded his return to a Swiss sanatorium where he stayed until the following winter. The period was marked emotionally by his realisation that the ecstatic connection with Gala, begun earlier at another sanatorium, was now riddled with anxiety, tension and anguish which could not be resolved or dispersed.

In 1929 Éluard's *L'Amour la poésie / Love and Poetry* was published. 'This endless text' was dedicated to Gala, its title having been poignantly suggested by their nine-year-old daughter whose parents were about to divorce. The work was marked by deep intractable shadows of doubt and nightmares of paralysis, as well as by images of the luminosity of loving and of its apogee. It traced as much an anxiety about the inability to sustain love as it did a celebration of love. That summer the couple accompanied Camille Goëmans and Magritte to Cadaquès in Spain to visit Salvador Dalí. The encounter of Gala and Dalí was one of engulfing passion, and Éluard left without her. The next years of work were marked by his inner unravelling of the powerful connection with Gala. He remained in passionate correspondence with her throughout the 1930s, despite the new daily focus of his own personal life – Maria Benz, the daughter of two acrobats from Alsace, known as Nusch, whom he met in 1930.

The Surrealist group, in the wake of Breton's Second Surrealist

Manifesto (1930), was weathering Bretonian excommunications, individual evacuations and a new influx of collaborators. The latter included Buñuel, Dalí, Sadoul, Hugnet, a returning Tzara, and René Char, who became a close, life-long friend to Éluard. April 1930 saw the publication by Éditions Surréalistes of *Ralentir travaux / Roadworks ahead*, an experimental collection of 30 poems Éluard wrote collaboratively with Breton and Char, and Éluard's own *À toute épreuve / Under all Duress*, a little sequence of poems dreaming around imaginary projections of desire, conflicting emotions and poignant images of solitude. *The Surrealist Revolution* was now renamed (under closer ties with the PCF which was unsympathetic to the independence of the Surrealist venture) as *Le Surréalisme au service de la révolution / Surrealism in the Service of Revolution*. At the same time, Éluard and Breton were pursuing their not particularly Marxist, but very Surrealist interest in automatic writing, exploring the workings of the unconscious and notions of language untrammelled by the controlling mechanisms of reason and social logic. They wrote together *L'Immaculée conception / The Immaculate Conception*, a prose text where their undifferentiated voices interweave, simulating various mental, socially 'deregulated' conditions as they associate poetic practice with delirious, paradoxical formulations, unbridled from the grammar of "normal" life.

Emotional and political transitions: the Nusch years

Aragon and Sadoul, after attending the Second International Conference of Revolutionary Writers at Kharkov in the Soviet Union, returned to Paris having unexpectedly signed a statement condemning the bourgeois decadence of Surrealism and its preoccupations with psychoanalysis. Back in Paris, confronted by fellow Surrealists, they recanted, but the polarising of Surrealism and the PCF, after the illusory lull of the seemingly viable 'marriage between the carp and the rabbit' (as Pierre Naville would call it later), was now relentlessly in motion. There was a co-ordinated effort from Surrealists and Communists together to mount an anti-colonial exhibition in Paris, opposing the official Colonial Exhibition that opened in 1931. Éluard and Aragon worked hard together on this project. All Éluard published that year was a private edition of *Dors / Go to Sleep*, though his signature did appear on several Surrealist tracts. Among these, *Ne visitez pas l'exposition coloniale / Stay away from the Colonial Exhibition* denounced the collaboration

17

of repressive regimes, the Catholic church, French bureaucracy and corporate interests in exploiting colonised countries; it called for the withdrawal of troops from the colonies and an indictment of 'generals and officials responsible for the massacres in Annam, Lebanon, Morocco and Central Africa'. *Au Feu! / Burn Them Down* was an anticlerical tract approving the phase of church burning in Spain. It accused the church of being invested in the interests of the bourgeoisie at the expense of the people. Another tract, however, condemned the arson which destroyed exhibits at the Colonial exhibition.

In the early 1930s, Éluard's personal life was oscillating between anguished withdrawal symptoms as he digested the definitive distancing from Gala, and a new sense of happiness and pleasure in his relationship with Nusch. He and Nusch spent much time with Char, Crevel, and Man Ray, travelling a lot, despite the fragility of his finances. After leaving employment with his father, Éluard never held another full-time job. Money he inherited on his father's death quickly slid through his fingers under his own mismanagement. Beyond that, he existed often on very little. The networks he moved in promoted a sharing of resources, a welcoming to each others' space for short or prolonged stays. Éluard, a committed bibliophile and amateur art collector (often highly perceptive in terms of contemporary talent and in touch with most artists of his time), survived at different times throughout his life by selling when he was broke, and purchasing when he had cash. Even up until his death he was often in debt, and his correspondence traces a continuous anxiety about money mixed with relief when his writing boosted his finances. He was also generous, sharing his resources with Gala long after their separation. He worried that Nusch was so totally dependent on his erratic income.

In June 1932 Éluard's *La Vie immédiate / The Immediacy of Life* was published, a moving poetic testimony to the disintegration of love, the destabilising sense of loss and solitude in the absence of the consenting, desired woman. It evoked

> Love of loveable bodies
> Power of love
> Whose loveability rises up
> Like a bodyless monster

and invented relief from absence

> I create relationships between man and woman...
> Between enchanted grottos and the avalanche...
> Between hollow eyes and wild laughter...
> Between horsehooves and fingertips...
> Between my solitude and you...

18

an absence where

> ...Solitude falsifies any presence
> One kiss just one more kiss a single one
> To stop thinking more about the desert

Poems to Breton, Crevel, Tanguy, Dalí, Ernst, Péret, Char and Nusch offset an invasive sense of loss against his nostalgic, insistent retracing of the rituals of his love for Gala. A poignant prose poem, 'Nuits partagées'/'Shared Nights', traces those problematic rituals of love, the 'conventional colours and forms which let me draw near to you', the tenderness, compulsive obsession and erotic fixations which framed the 'discord of presence and the harmony of absence...the science of deprivations'. It questions the fictions he saw himself imposing on 'dreadful realities', the empty houses his imagination peopled with 'women made always more seductive than possible by one single detail' to sustain his desire; it is concerned with the nausea of the problematic rituals ushering in the ending of love. This text was published on its own in 1935, with illustrations by Dalí, now Gala's partner. The collection ended abruptly by juxtaposing the representational dilemmas of the desired/desirable/desiring man and woman with the problem of the relationship beween poetry and politics, the reader and the desired/desirable/desiring poet. 'Critique de la poésie' / 'Criticism of Poetry' stood starkly at the end of the book, a provocative poem challenging and indicting a readership more prone to admiration of love poetry (assumed to be apolitical) than to digesting an explicit, rebellious, political stance taken by the poet:

> Of course I hate the reign of the bourgeoisie
> The reign of cops and priests
> But I hate even more whoever doesn't hate it
> Like I do
> With every ounce of strength
>
> I spit in the face of the stunted little man
> Who of all my poems does not prefer this *Criticism of Poetry*

The crisis on the political and cultural terrain now intensified. Aragon was defended by the Surrealists against police accusations of incitement to murder over his poem *Front Rouge / Red Front*. After wavering, he rejected their defence, claimed the subversive, 'realist' militancy of the text and abandoned Surrealism to centre himself definitively in the PCF. Éluard signed the collective text condemning Aragon, and his own *Certificat / Certificate* denounced Aragon's waverings and betrayal, quoting Lautréamont: 'All the water in the sea would never suffice to wash out a single intellectual bloodstain'. The international, anti-war Congrès d'Amsterdam-Pleyel, attended by Éluard with other Surrealists, marked another stage of the critical distance between them and the PCF. Éluard signed the Surrealist tract protesting against the French government's refusal of political asylum to Trotsky. By the end of 1933, Éluard, Breton and Crevel were excluded from the PCF over refusals to denounce Dalí's work as pornographic, to condemn articles and stances critical of the USSR and over the lapse of active involvement in their Party branches. *Minotaure* was now the new Surrealist publication, to which Éluard contributed until 1938. With both Picasso and Lacan now figuring among its contributors, it had a more aesthetic and psychoanalytical bias and was to lean away from the political concerns that had marked earlier Surrealist publications.

Hitler was now in full ascendency in Germany. Following right-wing riots in Paris and a French general strike, Éluard signed pamphlets calling for unified opposition to mounting Fascism in France. In August 1934 he married Nusch. December saw the publication of his new, emotionally complex work, *La Rose publique / Public Rose*, a Surrealist apogee of condensed imagery, disorientating in relation to more accessible, familiar terms of poetic narrative logic. It was also haunted by images of disillusionment and of adulterated ideals:

> The most familiar systems crack in the gloved hands of prisons
> Gleaming movements are extinguished there shadows accrue...
> Like slow motion deer tamed broken in
> They accept chains as limits
> Cultivate happiness skills
> Leaning now and then on the complacent lever of property
> They dilute their own sunlight

In March 1935, Breton and Éluard, hosted by Toyen and Nezval, attended the Prague Surrealist Exhibition, giving a series of talks, readings and interviews. On Czech radio they asserted: 'Today art that is authentic sides with action promoting social revolution, wanting, like it, the destruction of capitalist society....'. This clarity of political position was argued simultaneously with their Surrealist cultural agenda: 'Fixed forms have had their day...The world is a trellis of echoes and images, in perpetual motion but where nothing is repeated.'

Back in Paris, plagued by continued tension with the PCF, the Surrealists were held at critical distance from participation in the PCF-backed Writers' Congress for the Defence of Culture. Tension was immense and shortly before the congress, for an apparent convergence of personal and political reasons, René Crevel, now a very close friend of Éluard, committed suicide. Emotions ran high. Breton was banned from attending the congress after a violent encounter with Ehrenbourg, where their differences were aggressively orchestrated by homophobic insults on both sides. On the day of the congress, Éluard read Breton's text to a generally unsympathetic, dwindling audience.

Through this political, cultural and personally traumatic turbulence, Éluard wrote *Facile / Easy*, a sequence of luminous love poems to Nusch. They appeared each framed intimately by Man Ray's erotically allusive photographs of her naked body (not without some scandalised response to Éluard's own wife's body being figured in this way), her image curved to the visual layout of the lines of poetry. This short book of poems marked the new terms of love emerging now for Éluard. The loved women and love itself stand not as a self-enclosed place of projected satiation and self-centred closure, as did the poems of the Gala years, but as a symbolic site of both sensual connection and wider, future desires; a site of potential human connection, and the hope for new visions. He wrote in *Easy*:

> We for ever
> Left behind us that hope wasted
> In a city riddled with flesh misery
> And tyranny...
> Our kisses and hands at our own level
> Way beyond all ruins
> Almond-shaped youth bares itself and dreams...
> Our shadow does not extinguish the fire
> We prolong each other...
>   ...And in my head gently balancing yours in the dark
> I marvel at the unknown woman you become
> A stranger resembling you and everything I love
> Constantly renewed...
> ...Here is where we defend our life
> Where we seek the world

Instead of a place for private turning into a claustrophobic zone of personal pleasure or damage, to be sifted through as a turning away from the world, love was now, even at its most poignant points of desire, a rallying point for larger emotions with the power to reshape an engaged, caring future.

The Surrealist position was now explicitly critical of the PCF and of Stalinism. The last two Surrealist tracts which Éluard was to participate in addressed this directly. *Du Temps que les surréalistes avaient raison / When the Surrealists Were Right* (1935) marked out strong reservations about blind trust in and dependence on the USSR, condemned the cult of Stalin, the repression of critical debate and censorship. Éluard supported both the Surrealist break with the PCF and the assertion of Surrealism's commitment to operating under the aegis of a revolutionary struggle opposed to capitalism and informed by democratic Marxism. What was involved in this was not a move away from left-wing politics and their critique of capitalism and colonialism, but a distancing from the disturbing forms into which Soviet Stalinism was shaping the communist project. A manifesto Éluard signed in October (attempting to found a non-communist organisation of revolutionary intellectuals) criticised PCF positions by altering key words in original PCF statements to give them opposing or heretical meanings. This was a subversive textual strategy that was repeated in *Notes sur la poésie / Notes on Poetry* which Breton and Éluard published in May 1936, where they quoted from Valéry's poetics, redirecting his intent by changing his own key words in the text.

Anti-fascist priorities

In the shaping of Éluard's evolving perspectives 1936 was a crucial year. After a winter spent in Switzerland for health reasons, 1936 began for him with a series of talks and readings in Spain, linked to a major Picasso retrospective which was shown in Barcelona, Madrid and Bilbão between January and March. This brought Éluard into contact with Spanish artists and writers, including García Lorca. He and Nusch travelled to England in May to stay with Roland Penrose, who was organising the London Surrealist exhibition and was to become Éluard's good friend over the ensuing years. In April Éluard published *Le Front couvert / The Veiled Mind*, a poem which associates negative images with disconnection and isolation, and stages the desire for a clearer agenda of involvement:

> Strong coral coldness
> Heart's shadow
> Dulls my eyes as they half open
> With no hold on fraternal dawn
> I want to sleep alone no more
> No more waking
> Drenched in sleep and dreams
> Not recognising light
> And life immediately

This leaning into the affirmation of solidarity, the need to be actively positioned with others in an attempt at political intervention, was to assume greater focus for him as the year advanced. His next work, *La Barre d'appui / Somewhere to Lean On*, dedicated to Nusch, with three watercolours by Picasso, traced images of violence and questioned passive complicity in repression. Friction with Breton increased during their collaboration over planning the London exhibition and nearly caused Éluard not to attend it. He did, however, read his personal Surrealist manifesto, *Évidence poétique / The Self-Evidence of Poetry*, in the June exhibition at the Burlington Galleries (now the ICA) in London. He stressed the Surrealist recognition that 'the relation between things is no sooner established than it is erased to let others, just as fleeting, occur... nothing can be sufficiently described, nothing reproduced literally'. The opening of his speech presented poets as 'deeply rooted in the lives of other men, in a shared life'. It paid tribute to Lautréamont, to Sade, and to their efforts to free the imagination by transgressing the boundaries of bourgeois conventions. His speech ended with anti-war sentiments, criticism of the terms which sustain bourgeois well-being and morality, and the claim that 'poets are now down in the streets... learning songs of revolt from the wretched crowd and trying to teach them theirs... they are now sure they speak for all'. The landscape he mapped out for poetry was one signposted by a provocative combination of Sade, Marx, Picasso, Rimbaud, Lautréamont and Freud. Éluard had a warm reception from David Gascoyne, Humphrey Jennings, Herbert Read and Henry Moore, who all found the exhibition inspirational.

In July, the Spanish Civil War broke out, with the advance of Franco's Fascist forces. Lorca was murdered in an early sweep of organised killing. Éluard's thoughts were focused on the massing of Fascist forces and he was not party to the Surrealists' protests against the repressive Moscow 'mock' trials. In October his book *Les Yeux fertiles / Fertile Eyes* was published, with its Picasso illustrations – series of dense poems, charged with contradictory images of enabled and disabled masculine desire, where invitations to intimacy and pleasure interweave with a claustrophobic sense of obstacle. In December his poem 'Novembre 1936' explicitly addressed the Spanish war and appeared in *L'Humanité*, significantly marking his now closer links with the Party.

In 1937 he participated in the Surrealist homage to Jarry – a performance of the play *Ubu enchaîné / Ubu Unchained*. He attended the Paris performance of nine of his own poems set to music by Poulenc (the first of seven works by Poulenc, over the next decades, to be based on Éluard's poems). He and Nusch spent time in Cornwall that summer, at Roland Penrose's house near Truro, where their time was interspersed with visits from Max Ernst, Leonora Carrington, Man Ray, Eileen Agar, Herbert Read, E.L.T. Mesens and Lee Miller. In November *Les Mains libres / With Free Hands* appeared subtitled 'drawings by Man Ray illustrated by the poems of Paul Éluard'; it is a powerful combination of over 50 drawings and enigmatic, brief texts, many of which suggest tension, suspended anxiety, risk and impossibility. That year saw new initiatives by Éluard, new reflections on poetic and artistic processes of representation. He read *Avenir de la poésie / The Future of Poetry*, his brief, condensed reflections on poetry, in Paris at a day colloquium at the International Exhibition at the Théâtre des Champs-Élysées. *Minotaure* published his *Premières vues anciennes / First Gaze Back* (a text later to be incorporated in his 1939 book *Donner à voir / Reasons for Seeing*). This was a series of thoughts about poetry, language, the imagination and representation, weaving Éluard's own ideas with extracts from other poets.

Éluard never attempted to write fully-fledged, theoretical treatises on poetics. He preferred to explore his ideas through a technique which he used in a variety of books in the 1940s, drawing widely on his own reading of others' texts to form a patchwork of extracted key ideas for the inspiration of the reader. He set angles of his own thoughts on writing and art in dialogue with words of a wide range of writers, artists and thinkers. December saw the publication of two short pieces. One was a Surrealist story, *Appliquée / Applied Woman*, a short prose piece about a feminine subject 'courting her image of herself'. It had earlier appeared illustrated by Man Ray and Hans Bellmer in *Minotaure* and was now illustrated by Valentine Hugo. The other was *Quelques-uns des mots qui jusqu'ici m'étaient mystérieusement interdits / Certain words mysteriously forbidden to me up until now*, a text playing with typeface and layout reminiscent of Apollinaire's play with textual layout; it ended with the words:

> o this my human empire
> these words I write here despite all evidence
> from my intense anxiety to say everything

This concern to give evidence, to bear witness to what needs witnessing, and to speak – somehow against all odds and with renewed effort of all that needs to be heard – is central to Éluard's work, and can be seen surfacing in *Unbroken Poetry II*. In January 1938 the highly successful Paris International Surrealist Exhibition opened, organised by Éluard and Breton. The text they prepared together for this was published at the end of the year as the *Dictionnaire abrégé du surréalisme / A Concise Dictionary of Surrealism.*

In March, Éluard's *Cours naturel / The Natural Way* was published, a versatile combination of poems leaning to the most personal, the most creative and the most political dimensions of his inspiration. In it 'Sans âge'/'Ageless' prefaced the reprinting of 'Novembre 1936' with the lines:

> The sky will widen
> We have had enough
> Of dwelling in ruins of sleep
> In low shadows of rest
> Of fatigue and abandonment
> The earth will take shape from our living bodies...
> Hands acknowledged by ours
> Lips merging with ours...
> Out from all caverns
> Out from our very selves

This movement would be one Éluard reiterated time and again: a move from complacency, from abstract meanderings of ideas, from passivity and lack of energy, from the games of the mind towards a body in action, connecting with others, taking a stand, intervening in unfolding events, affirming human agency. Love needed a re-scripted landscape. Tender lines tracing intimacy and desire had to relate to more solemn reminders:

> Let us not forget the nightingale
> Nor the chess game hidden in the sand
> Nor the bones of the dead
> Nor the suspended dead leaves
> Of eternal December

Images of the feminine object of desire stood side by side with others which questioned 'the solid bases of man and woman'. 'Le tableau noir'/'The Blackboard' (dedicated to Léonore Fini, a Surrealist painter whose work depicted a powerful, woman-centred erotic) evoked desire, beautified women destroyed by men's kisses, humiliated, saddened and pained by men they now turn their backs on, seeking other women rather than men ensconced in positions of conventional masculinity. Other poems staged authoritarian, solitary and indifferent men, unable to see that their 'woman garden house' was as 'miserable as any other', while in 'Paroles peintes'/ 'Painted Words', dreams of a multiple, all-inclusive poetic project, grounded beyond self-centred preoccupations, gave rise to questions of how to

> ...give the thoughtful lone woman
> The form of caresses
> She dreams of for herself

Heavy, dark texts laced with paralysis and inertia stand by others with a socially critical gaze, asking:

> On what wall am I engraving myself...
> On what slope do I stand
> What sap rises in me
> Where are the ruins inspiring me
> To live despite all ruins

Éluard persisted in questioning the stakes of his own subjective stance, sifting through the contradictions and tensions within the moment when a provisionally coherent subject 'speaks'. He meets head-on the dilemmas of an apparently stable self which in fact can only speak in order to question the place it speaks from. His poetry was recurrently haunted, on different levels, by re-evaluations of the poetic subject and of the discourses which define its positions.

His poem 'La Victoire de Guernica'/'The Guernica Victory' was finished alongside Picasso as he worked on his famous painting following the military annihilation of the Spanish village by the Fascist airforce. They were exhibited together (just as they are housed together today in their specially allocated building near the Prado museum in Madrid) in the Spanish pavilion of the 1937 Paris International Exhibition. *The Natural Way* was followed by *Solidarité / Solidarity*, a special offprint of 'November 1936', with engravings by Picasso, Miró, Tanguy, Masson and others, which was sold as a fund-raiser for Republican forces in Spain. Within this anti-fascist activism, Éluard's poem 'Facile proie'/'Easy Prey', its images inditing indifference and self-satisfied illusions of immunity, was published on its own, illustrated by S.W. Hayter, and Éluard and Louis Parrot published their translation of Lorca's *Ode à Salvador Dalí*.

That year Breton met Trotsky and Diego Rivera in Mexico, and tried, again unsuccessfully, to launch an international organisation of independent revolutionary writers. Éluard, overwhelmingly preoccupied with advancing Fascism in Europe, was, however, finding increasingly more in with common people he knew in the PCF. From 1936 his relationship with Breton grew ever more tense. The difficulties they had had preparing the London Surrealist exhibition together now resurfaced as they collaborated over the

1938 one in Paris. Breton's continuing papal-like pronouncements on the movement and its individual members were aggravating to many of the Surrealists. Breton now gave central priority to opposition to the communist parties and the implications of their Stalinism. Éluard, though anti-Stalinist in ideas, was sceptical of the truth behind anti-communist criticism, as indeed many left-wing intellectuals were until the mid 1950s. He was coming to see the PCF as the most viable option, the most important force of opposition to mounting Fascism. His affinity with the Party infuriated Breton. Their definitive break that year was recorded by Éluard as a highly personal rupture, marking his final impatience with Breton's dictates and arrogance. Breton narrated it as a polemically ideological break, pontificating later that Éluard never was a 'true Surrealist', claiming erroneously that he had published in Fascist journals, and depicting his link with the Party as a deep identification with the repressions of Stalinism itself. Éluard, while distancing himself from Breton's imposed agendas, never denounced Surrealism. He maintained a dynamic relationship to its tenets over the ensuing years, as is demonstrated in texts such as the 1949 *Les Sentiers et les routes de la poésie / The Highways and Byways of Poetry*, and many poems sustaining the mode of expression evolved by him in the Surrealist heyday. In the actual political contexts he was facing he also now wrote poems which were linked to a more identifiable social immediacy, which were at times more accessible than those of his texts that were laced with Surrealist disruptions. His work was more and more affected by an agenda of social involvement and at times prioritised more direct, occasional, cultural and political interventions. Breton tried at this time to mount a Surrealist boycott of Éluard. Hugnet, Char and Ernst, finding Breton's stand ridiculous, refused to denounce Éluard; feelings ran high and they were 'expelled' by Breton. Man Ray, Penrose, Mesens, Hayter, Duchamp, Magritte, Arp, Bellmer, Matta, Miró and Picasso were among Surrealists who did not feel that their positive connection with Éluard was affected by his break with Breton.

In 1939 four new works by Éluard appeared, as well as a collection of Baudelaire's writings which he selected and introduced. *Chanson complète / The Finished Song* appeared in a limited, deluxe edition with lithographs by Ernst. In it poems balance ideas of love and commitment, questioning the frontiers dividing the realms of the conscious and unconscious mind (one poem is entitled 'NO RUPTURE light and consciousness swamp me with as much mystery and unhappiness as do night and dreams'). Several poems suggest criticism of withheld commitment, of postures of self-importance and collusion through passivity, and can be read significantly in the light of the break with Breton. The year saw publication of two connected but vividly contrasting collaborative projects, both addressing the topography of the female body, the desired/desiring terrain of the feminine object. With Valentine Hugo he published *Médieuses / Feminine Gods*, where his poems were juxtaposed with her lithographs of women's bodies prepared under detailed specifications; the book was an attempt to invent 'a kind of feminine mythology'. With Hans Bellmer he published the first version of their *Jeux vagues de la poupée / Vague games with the doll*, which came to be seen as a "classic" of Surrealist erotica. This was a combination of brief texts by Éluard tracing a mobile deciphering of the feminine object of desire beside photographs of Bellmer's famous doll – an arrangement of naked, female torso and limbs in disconcerting, provocative combinations. Dismemberment and impossibly arranged limbs created a disturbing sense of complex erotic tension charged by the male gaze.

Reasons for Seeing (June 1939), a work of great significance to Éluard himself, was comprised of distinct sections juxtaposing prose poems, dream texts, abstract reflections on poetry, painting and representation with reflections and quotations on writing and poetry, and poems written by him to individual painters. Musing on the 'signs in motion' of art and its 'assembling, deconstruction and reconstruction' of meaning, Éluard emphasised the inevitable presence of 'ideas of value', and that 'any true morality is poetic, since poetry tends towards the reign of man, of all men, the reign of our justice'. The poetic self is at stake in the production of meanings, since verbal and visual texts are predicated on arrangements of sign systems, and make their interventions in terms of the imagination and subjective positionings which prioritise certain perspectives, certain values, certain constructed interpretations. 'A truly materialist interpretation of the world,' Éluard wrote here, 'cannot exclude from that world the human being observing it.' He claimed absolute freedom, of artistic method, while combing through the ways in which that freedom was itself ideologically articulated, and insisting on the deepest sense of responsibility inherent in every act of creativity. Éluard worked to sustain a productive tension in relation to, but decentred from, what were for him the equally untenable poles of communist framed social realism and the ultimately co-optable aestheticism of Surrealist experimentation.

War, resistance and communism

When war was declared in September 1939, Éluard was called up and stationed to work on supplies south of Paris. Nusch stayed nearby, and he completed *Le Livre ouvert / The Open Book*, a collection of poems on love and the power of hope, but laced with images of war and apprehension. He successfully ensured Max Ernst's release from a foreigners' military camp. Following the emergence of the Vichy government, the Armistice signed with Hitler and the German occupation of Paris, Éluard returned to Paris to find many of his friends had left. His pre-Occupation poems came into print: *Blason des fleurs et des fruits / Emblems of Fruits and Flowers*, illustrated by Valentine Hugo; *Moralité du sommeil / Morality of Sleep*, illustrated by Magritte. These moved between images of anxiety at the external 'derisory disorder' and towards a claimed coherence based in intimacy with the loved woman. In the face of the uncertainties of war, 'she' was posited as the site of any possible survival and inspiration. His *Choix de poèmes / Selected Poems* (October 1941) anthologised a selection of his writings from all the years of his work. It was as if war, with its risk of sudden death, urged a survey of his achievements. *Sur les pentes inférieures / On the Lower Slopes* traced images of killing and repulsion in 'this the most ugly of springtimes', while intimacy and desire were no longer places of personal evasion and comfort, but inspiration for revenge and solidarity.

Early in 1942 Éluard published *Le Livre ouvert II / Open Book II* and *La Dernière nuit / That Final Night*. These were occasional poems, but of an unusual kind, with no direct naming of the Nazis; they marked out explicitly the 'ravaging thirst' for freedom, the indictment of repression and violence, those 'mirrors misted over with inhumanity' and drew readers towards resistance:

> And the vaguest cloud
> The most ordinary word
> Lost objects
> Make them all take wing
> Make them like your heart
> Have them serve everything that lives

His poems spelled out the crimes:

> They had skinned his hands broken his back
> Blown a hole in his head

and invoked a response to promote retaliation as well as liberation:

I can hear plottings
Of dimensions multiplied by future strength...
...We throw the burden of shadows in the fire
We break rusty locks of injustice
Men of the future will fear for themselves no more

These moments of insistence on the global potential of human values to counter the dehumanising landscape of Nazism, and his call for the urgent mobilisation of resistance, would resurface throughout Éluard's wartime writing. The PCF had been banned by the Nazis. Communists and Jews headed the Nazi hit-list. It was now, in the context of the imperatives of resistance, that Éluard rejoined the PCF, and reformulated his communist position in alliance with his imagery of hope and desire. He let the rumour circulate that he was Jewish. A new book of poems, *Poésie et vérité 1942 / Poetry and Truth 1942*, again poignantly evoked the claustrophobia of curfews, imprisonment, betrayal and fear, insistently turning to love for the energy to survive and will to resist. It was distributed rapidly through both the occupied and the free zones of France. Circulating via Portugal, Switzerland, Algeria and Belgium, *Poetry and Truth 1942* reached England and the RAF parachuted thousands of copies over the occupied zones.

Éluard was now named a public enemy by the Nazis. He went into hiding in Paris, changing his home base frequently to avoid arrest. During 1943 he worked with the new underground press, Éditions de Minuit. His Paris network included Vercors, Paulhan, Leiris, Desnos, Zervos, Parrot, Scheler and Seghers. Éluard organised the Northern section of a national writers' committee, and helped prepare and distribute anthologies of Resistance poetry. This work led him to a warm reconciliation with Louis Aragon and Elsa Triolet. Seghers published Éluard's *Poésie involontaire et poésie intentionelle / Involuntary and Unintentional Poetry*, which rapidly sold out. It was a selection of quotations from writers as varied as Dickens, Michaux, Kafka, Synge, Cervantes, Lacan and Lautréamont among many others, and gestured in varied and surprising ways towards the 'absolute freedom of the word' and the belief that, for the poet, 'from the world imposed on him is born the world he dreams of'. This strategy of juxtaposing extracts from the thoughts and creative texts of other writers alongside his own words was one Éluard found productive. It put his voice in dialogue with other voices, made his poetic project part of other continuing explorations, and linked his linguistic, moral and political agendas to a wide itinerary made up of a range of thinkers. Meanwhile, in 1943, he worked tirelessly with Decour and Paulhan to produce clandestine issues of *Les Lettres françaises*. While in hiding for some months in a psychiatric hospital, his *Sept poèmes d'amour en guerre / Seven War-time Love Poems* came out under a pseudonym distributed by the clandestine press networks. It placed the desire for freedom in a dynamic relation to the human capacity for connection, itself framed and supported by erotic desire:

> Because we love each other
> We would free others
> From their frozen solitude...
>   ...we want
> Light to perpetuate
> Couples gleaming with virtue
> Couples armoured with daring
> Because they look into each other's eyes
> While their goal lies in the lives of others

In Paris in February 1944, he collaborated on secret recordings, edited a further Resistance anthology and founded the underground *L'Éternelle Revue / The Eternal Review* with his close friend Louis Parrot. His *Pour vivre ici / To Go on Living Here* appeared through Belgium. *Le Lit la table / The Bed the Table* was printed in Switzerland, and included poems, such as 'À celle qui répète ce que je dis'/'For the woman who repeats my words', which mapped a trajectory from disarray and paralysis to determined engagement, from drifting randomness to discovered direction, and which celebrated the presence of love. These strategic connections were to be keystones of his poetic vision over the eight final years of his life, and were forerunners to the two volumes of *Unbroken Poetry*. Echoing the challenge which ended *Immediacy of Life* years before with a poem of the same title, this volume concluded with a second 'Critique de la poésie'/'Criticism of Poetry', where upward energies of aesthetic beauty and images generating hope are disrupted sparsely by single lines naming the 'Nazi assassinations' of Lorca, Saint-Pol-Roux, Decour. Éluard continued to contest literary dogmas which depoliticised the personal, "love text" landscape, marginalised social reality within the field of poetry, and threatened in this way to undermine its legitimacy. He took up this theme later in his 1947 poem ' "La poésie doit avoir pour but la vérité pratique" '/ ' "Poetry must have as its goal practical truth" ' (a quotation from Lautréamont). *Les Armes de la douleur / The Arms of Grief* and *Dignes de vivre / Worthy of Living* (a reprint of *Poetry and Truth*) came into circulation before the liberation of Paris in August 1944. His *Rendez-vous allemand / German Rendezvous* came out at the end of the year and was reprinted, each time with expanded content, three times in the next two years. In December *À Pablo Picasso / To Pablo Picasso*, published in Switzerland, combined thirty-seven former texts by Éluard dedicated to Picasso's work, with thirty paintings by Picasso selected by the two of them. His passionate, collaborative, intimate friendship with Picasso spanned some twenty years.

Post-war agendas and new traumas

1945 saw the publication four books: *En avril 1944: Paris respirait encore / April 1944: Paris still breathing* with Jean Hugo's watercolours; *Lingères légères / Light Linen Maids* headed by a portrait by Marcoussis; and two selections from his earlier poems, *Doubles d'ombre / Shadow Doubles*, illustrated by André Beaudin, and *Une Longue réflexion amoureuse / Prolonged Thoughts on Love*, which opened with a portrait by Picasso of Nusch. Travelling with Nusch and Claude Roy, Éluard gave talks in England and Switzerland. His first *Poésie ininterrompue / Unbroken Poetry* came out in January 1946. Its long dialectical title-poem moved from an ahistorical, adjectival, incantatory and private arrangement of desire, with shiftings between feminine and masculine voices to a repossessing of the world, a reassessment of the past and the power

> ...one morning emerging from a dream...
> To make good of life...
> And organise the disaster

Love was reframed within the poem as a conscious participant in something larger than its usual narrative trajectory:

> But from pledged happiness beginning with two of us
> The first word
> Already forms confident refrains
> Against fear and hunger
> A sign to rally...

> Let my word weigh against the passing darkness
> And let the door keep opening
> Through which you entered this poem
> Door of your smile door of your body

> By you I move from light to light
> Warmth to warmth
> Through you I speak and you stay at the centre
> Of everything like sunlight consenting to gladness

But we must turn our clear eyes a little longer
Towards that inhuman darkness
Of men who didn't find life on earth
We must qualify their fate to save them

We will start from below and from above...

Critically alluding to and re-assessing various contexts of cultural, social and personal priorities, the poem expresses the sensation of rising towards a freedom where

Mumbled alphabets
Of histories and morals
And submissive syntax
Of taught memory
Gradually decompose

and the sexual couple is reconstructed as a collective subject central to the project of being 'faithful to life'. 'Le Travail du poète'/ 'The Task of the Poet' traces a journey from pointless, enigmatic verbal games to a vision of loving both intense and personal, and enabling desire to turn to social awareness and connection. Poems to Picasso and Char affirm deep friendships and their significance for the creative process, and 'À l'Échelle animale'/ 'On the Animal Scale' presaged, with its use of animal imagery highlighting the borders of human consciousness, the angst to come in 'Blason dédoré de mes rêves'/'Tarnished Emblems of my Dreams', translated in this volume.

In April 1946 Éluard left for Czechoslovakia to give talks on poetry in Prague and Bratislava, before travelling on to Italy where he was welcomed in Milan and Rome to speak at the French Institute, in various Italian cultural circles and in factories. He went to Athens and Salonika visiting the freedom fighters in the hills, returned to visit Picasso in the South of France with Nusch, then travelled with her to Naples. Back in France, he received endless invitations to give talks and readings, and a flow of correspondence from readers. He turned down the Légion d'honneur which was offered to him. In November *Le Dur désir de durer / The Difficult Desire to Last* came out. Poems illustrated by Chagall again associate extraordinary tenderness, the effort to emerge from negativity and the will to write. *Objet des mots et des images / Object of Words and Images*, with Engel Pak's lithographs, was published just as his life took an unexpected and traumatic turn.

He was in Switzerland when Nusch died in Paris from a sudden brain haemorrhage. He rushed back to Paris, where René Char stayed with him for three days and nights as he mourned over Nusch's body. In unbearable despair, haunted by guilt from the pain which the 'free arrangement' of their relationship had at times been causing Nusch, Éluard went into a profound agony of depression. Jacqueline and Alain Trutat, friends who had been intimately involved with him and Nusch, took him into their home, and, helped also by other friends, they saw him through the worst period of his crisis, wracked with emotional pain. In 1947 *Le Temps déborde / Time Overflows* was published, under a pseudonym, a moving collection of poems pre- and post-dating Nusch's death, framed by exquisite portraits of her by Dora Maar and Man Ray. Within months, however, his real name came into print again with *Corps mémorable / Memorable Body*, dedicated to Jacqueline and celebrating the life-giving power of erotic desire. It marked Éluard's re-entry into writing after a year's impasse of impossibility and paralysis, and moved him into highly productive years of writing. His intimacy with Alain and Jacqueline, as well as his passionate involvement with a trapeze artist Diane de Riaz (whom he considered marrying) were of key importance to him in these years. His opening to the later *Poèmes politiques / Political Poems* was not what one would have expected under that title, charting as it did a rebirth from the edge of suicide and utter despair to political potential, through a sensuality indifferent to the social codes of marriage, monogamy and perhaps even to the limits of conventional heterosexuality:

> Those who loved him wound their hair, not their minds, around his madness...They represented, obstinately, a holding onto life...While he dreamed of being buried, deep in horror, brimming with absence, his heart in death, with living spectres of negativity...They shared their hunger, their bread, their embraces and caresses, their pure brows and confidence...And, mediated by the senses, gradually solidarity was reborn. One man friend, one woman friend and the world begins again, and formless matter takes shape...What have moralisers to do with any of this? A single man had been restored to his fellow beings as a legitimate brother...Let me judge for myself what helps me live.

Éluard's work now moved simultaneously in several directions. His connections with earlier Surrealists – Tzara, Ernst, Aragon, Picasso, Char, Sadoul, Hugnet – were very alive. His poetry framed a new volume of reproductions of Chagall's work. In early 1948 a collaborative publication of Ernst's earlier drawings with Éluard's new poems, *À l'Intérieur de la vue: Huit poèmes visibles / Inside Sight: Eight visible poems*, appeared. This work frequently evoked imagery of disillusionment, personal disablement and an inability to say what the situation called for – all newly articulated elements in the emotional field of his 'political', poetic discourse:

> All the faces were closed. Under taut, flawless skin the skull's bitter fruit was ripening its capital grimace. I wanted to sing of the shadows, to preside over chaotic transactions of decay, huge councils of poison, the roots' last convulsions, dying adolescence. But I stumbled on a pebble and my song petered out, stupefied.

His *Picasso, bon maître de la liberté / Picasso, fine master of freedom*, written while Michel Sima photographed Picasso at work at Antibes, accompanied the publication of a hundred of his photographs. *Voir / Seeing* was also published in 1948. Each of Éluard's poems in this collection was coupled with art work by one of the following: Picasso, Chagall, Gris, Villon, Léger, Klee, Braque, Chirico, Ernst, Miró, Tanguy, Masson, Beaudin, Magritte, Dalí, Penrose, Fini, Valentine Hugo, Balthus, Delvaux, Dora Maar, Dominguez, Ubac, Labisse, Cicero Días, Dubuffet, Hayter, Vulliamy, Chastel. It gave renewed, striking evidence of how unusually prolific Éluard's collaborations were, throughout his whole life, with a wide range of artists and writers. His particularly close friendship and collaborative relationship with Picasso had begun in 1936. Between then and 1952 some sixteen publications saw their work emerging out of this relationship. Either illustrations by Picasso figured in Éluard's collections of poetry; or Éluard wrote texts on Picasso for exhibition catalogues of the painter's work. They spent their summers together in 1936, 1937 and 1938. They were in close contact in Paris during the war. Éluard often went to write at Picasso's studio and he attended the readings of Picasso's mock Surrealist play, *Le Désir attrapé par la queue / Desire caught by the Tail* at Leiris's house in 1943. Éluard was undoubtedly influential in Picasso's decision to join the PCF in 1944. In the post-war period they travelled together to many international congresses, and spent most summers together in the south of France. They shared a certain kind of optimism about the linking of art to wide possibilities of social change, and their relationship was marked by pleasurable familiarity as well as a strong love and respect for each other's work.

Éluard was also engrossed now in sifting the past, attentively recapitulating where his work had taken him, gathering in the threads of his poetic itineraries – both through his own writing and that of others. At the end of 1947 he published *Le Meilleur choix de poèmes est celui que l'on fait pour soi (1818-1918) / The Best Selected Poems Are the Ones You Choose Yourself (1818-1918)*, an unusual range of poetic texts selected from extensive reading, destabilising the status quo of canonised "great texts", bringing together pieces by some thirty writers including Chateaubriand, Nerval, Lautréamont, Rimbaud, Verlaine, Laforgue, Saint-Pol-Roux, Jarry, Maeterlinck, Apollinaire, Bataille, Valéry, Fargue, Spire, Jacob, Cendrars and Reverdy. He intended this to be followed by a volume of selections from 15th-17th century poets and another of international poets. He wrote his own *Bestiaire/Bestiary*, published with watercolours by Roger Chastel, linking his work to Philippe de Thaun and 'the long line of moralist poets and storytellers who use animals to criticise and teach men'. It was also now that he published *Premiers poèmes / Early Poems*, his own earlier work from 1913 to 1921. 1948 also saw the appearance of *Political Poems*, a collection structurally echoing *Time Overflows* in that it assembled texts written before and after Nusch's death. Some of Éluard's most explicitly "occasional" and directly "simple", most prosaic poems (e.g. 'À mes camarades imprimeurs'/'To my comrades, the printers', 'À la mémoire de Paul Vaillant-Couturier'/'In memory of Paul Vaillant-Couturier', 'Strasbourg XIe congrès'/'The Strasbourg 11th Congress') are found in this work. But it was again a work in which love and its relevance to solidarity were central to a political vision:

> You who were the sensitive conscience of my flesh
> You I love forever who invented me
> You could not bear oppression nor contempt
> Your song dreamed of happiness on earth
> You dreamed of being free and I am prolonging you

After Aragon's preface, the opening text 'De l'horizon d'un homme à l'horizon de tous'/'From the horizon of one man to the horizon of all' traced Éluard's logic of the connection between the personal and the political in alternating prose and poetic narrative. This collection was followed by the publication of *Perspectives / Perspectives*, containing new poems on engravings by Albert Flocon. These texts are an intricate weave of contradictory meanings held in simultaneous tension by the play of perspective, and a sense of temporary verbal grasp on impossible, ambivalent representations.

Éluard became involved at this time with solidarity groups opposed to US McCarthyism and went on to campaign actively on behalf of the Rosenbergs, who were widely understood by the European Left to be victims of McCarthyist, anti-communist hysteria. He was refused entry to the United States to attend a conference at which he was listed to speak in 1948. With Picasso he attended the Wroclaw Peace Congress in Poland, relaxing in Switzerland en route home with the Trutats. As a member of the communist-sponsored World Peace Council, he was an active delegate at its Paris conference in 1949, where Picasso's dove of peace appeared on the delegate cards. *Léda / Leda* was published with a sequence of drawings by Géricault tracing the move from feminine innocence to awareness and a full, assertive sensuality embodied in the mythological figure Leda. *La Saison des amours / Seasons of Loving* reprinted poems from his 1932 *Immediacy of Life*, with watercolours by Friedlander, appeared before Éluard left for Macedonia with Yves Fargue in April. There he spent time with Markos's Resistance fighters on Mt Grammos, and, under their armed protection, addressed, in simultaneous translation through two hundred loudspeakers, the monarchist, Fascist forces in combat against them. Back in France his poem 'Athena', illustrated by Picasso, was sold as a fund-raiser for the Committee for Solidarity with Democratic Greece. A first edition of his *Grèce ma rose de raison / Greece My Rose of Reason*, with wood-carvings by Srnitch, was followed by a second edition including translated poems by the executed Greek, Yannopoulos. In July he was invited back to his birthplace, St Denis, to take part in the ceremony inaugurating the installation of canvases by Amblard and a statue of Robespierre. Then he was on the move once more, accompanied again by the Trutats – meeting up with Pablo Neruda at the Budapest centenary tributes to Petöfi. In September 1949, after publishing *Je l'aime elle m'aimait / I love her she loved me*, a short poem dedicated to Jacqueline, written in the oppositional format of juxtaposed sections of 'right' and 'wrong' which he now often employed, Éluard left as a delegate for the World Peace Council to attend its congress in Mexico.

At the Mexico Congress he met Dominique Laure, who now became his inseparable companion. A former law student, she had worked for the French airforce in North Africa during the war. Firmly socialist, she was a sometime fellow-traveller to the communist milieu, while remaining critically sceptical of the defensive Stalinist communist vision in Cold War France. She was a determined, 'instinctively feminist', strongly independent woman in her mid-thirties, some twenty years younger than Éluard. She had already been married twice. Her first marriage had taken place as a student in Bordeaux (where she began a life long friendship with fellow student Claude Roy) and its story is illustrative of the characteristic boldness and non-traditional approach to life of the woman Éluard now fell in love with. In their student days, she and a homosexual friend decided to marry in order to navigate their ways out of dependency on controlling parents. Leaving the ceremony in their new, family-wedding-gift car, they waved good-bye to relatives before travelling off to meet their respective lovers for separate, somewhat unconventional honeymoons. They returned together and lived together amicably for a "respectable" period, before quietly seeking divorce. Her daughter Caroline was born from her second marriage to a doctor, whom she had divorced a few years before the encounter with Éluard in Mexico.

They returned to Paris shortly before the publication of *Une Leçon de morale* / *A Lesson in Morals*, a collection of poems still anchored by the loss of Nusch – the very structure of the work marks tension and contradiction. Most of the poems juxtapose a section leaning to 'le mal'/'wrong' (with connotations of pain in Éluard's use of the word) and another towards 'le bien'/right (a term which, usually coming second, recuperates affirmatively the feelings of negativity, disillusionment, loss and collapse found in each first section). The format displays all-pervasive, insistent doubt and despair; recurrent images of adulterated ideals and a decaying vision of possibilities open each poem. Having invested himself so passionately in Communism throughout the Resistance, having depended on it affectively after the traumatic loss of Nusch, Éluard was now haunted by growing criticisms on the French Left of the landscape of Communism. Dominique, in a 1985 interview, recalls how charged and impossible it was at this time to discuss the USSR, or Stalinism, or the problematic positions of the Party with Éluard in any calm way. He would explode with uncontrollable rage over their disagreements. Although not explicitly naming such questions, it is striking that Éluard's writings of the last few years of his life often work against a sense of moral disarray and suggest the loss of simpler, easier visions of right and wrong which the anti-Fascist struggle had enabled earlier in the 40s. The prose pieces of the preface to *A Lesson in Morals* evoke the disintegration of easy moral categories, a sense of ambivalently changing perspective, and a gnawing anxiety about the positioning of the poetic subject. Nusch's death emerges as highly specific and intimate; it is also symbolic of a loss of confidence and hope. This ambivalence is anticipated in the famous poem 'Liberté'/'Liberty':

> ...my sensitivity is already out of date...my blood often freezes... At the crossroads, right at the pivot, I held in my eyes a dead body, her – dead, my death... A sententious voice has been dictating to me ever since that from sorrow happiness becomes a postulate, but pessimism a vice. It carelessly adds that we need all truths to make a world...I started out with a conqueror's mentality. I was a new man. I was able to hold out before me a cloudless future. And if the suns I revelled in have been

destroyed by countless nights, if I have not triumphed, I have retained some notion of it. And despite everything, out of sorrow, danger or terror, I was able to spell out black and white reasons for hope...I imagined the inaccessible, constant life, happiness...I wanted to deny and eliminate black suns of illness and misery, nights of brine, cess-pools of shadows and chance, bad sight, blindness, destruction, dried blood, graves. Even if I only ever had one single moment of hope in my whole life, I would have fought that fight. Even if I must lose, for others will win.

These poems charted a vision dominated by ruins, where images emerge of 'a new order...of deformed foliage', 'at the heart of that which dies unopened', 'with horrifying wounds staining with blood' beneath the 'foundations of sunlight'. This is self-consciously offset by Éluard's familiar, insistent renewal and prolongation of desire, by which 'banks of love are banks of justice' and the feminine love object regenerates symbolically the body politic of the poet. Other texts reflect on the illusions of meaning invested in an arrangement of the feminine, and judge problematic the male poet's construction of 'his own architecture' in terms of projections of masculinity. *A Lesson in Morals* is particularly striking in its sifting of subjective positioning, its qualification of the tendency to simplicity (so often eulogised or condemned as the 'core' of Éluard's poetic project), its representation of desire as complex and the effort of political change as difficult. 'I had undertaken a huge emotional journey,' he wrote, 'when everything was against me.' Emphasising the explicitly political field of this work, the last poem, 'Tout est sauvé'/'All is Saved', was republished soon after on its own, accompanied by painfully graphic drawings of human anguish and suffering by the Jewish artist Mendjizki, under the title *Hommage aux martyrs et aux combattants du Ghetto de Varsovie / Tribute to the martyrs and fighters of the Warsaw Ghetto*.

Cold War options

In October and December 1949 Éluard, with several actors, presented five radio pieces based on his manscript eventually published in 1952 as *Les Routes et les sentiers de la poésie / The Highways and By-ways of Poetry*. This was a retrospective recapitulation of the terrain of poetry which, he said, took him 'twenty-five years and three months' to compose. Voices staged arguments about the concerns of poetry, the creative force of the imagination, the power of desire, and quoted, in the midst of Éluard's own script, the poems and writings of others to create a somewhat Surrealist array and at times 'absurd-style' juxtaposition of ideas, illustrations, stories, letters, laments and claims. Its aim was to generate a sense of the diversity of the terms of aesthetic debates, and to reflect on the ideological power of language. It framed, in a mosaic of creative fragments, questions concerning the moral resonance and responsibilities of creative intervention, the complex creativity of love, the importance of the landscapes of childhood and of its pre-logical grasp on the world, and the potential tranformations opened up by the unlimited freedom of the imagination.

In April 1950, with Dominique, Éluard visited Sofia, Prague (where they saw the Mayakovsky exhibition), and then, in May, Moscow, Stalingrad and Leningrad. Dominique had strong reservations about what they saw in the Soviet Union ('If you were not communist before you went there, there was nothing to see there that would convert you to communism,' she said in an interview). On their return home, Éluard railed defensively against her scepticism. He even announced to their friends, after one intense argument where she contested his over-simplified admiration for Soviet achievements, that they were splitting up. His rage settled fast however. He was passionately attached to her, and it is probable that her scepticism affected him so strongly because of his own latent, gnawing doubts about Soviet Stalinism. These were surfacing in the tension of his imagery, even if they were, as yet, unable to be articulated rationally in his daily life. Éluard dismissively swept aside Breton's public challenge to him in his 'Open Letter to Paul Éluard', where Breton appealed polemically, out of the vacuum of their estrangement, for his support against Stalin's staging of fixed trials to eliminate his critics and opponents.

Virulent anti-communism in France (escalating to cover up evidence of right-wing, war-time collusion with the Nazis) and pro-American, pro-Marshall plan, pro-capitalist configurations of the Right reinforced the loyalty of many to a communism they had experienced vividly in its Popular Front, anti-Nazi phase. There was a great complexity in the emotional tenor of these years, in the nature of the tensions surrounding political choices of position and allegiance. The mood of the time is perhaps best indicated to contemporary readers by registering that even the critical Jean-Paul Sartre, permanently sceptical of the costs of the Soviet path and of the policies it generated, came close to actually joining the PCF in 1952. By the end of 1956, after Khrushchev's speech indicting the repression and personality cult of the Stalin years, and in the midst of the Soviet invasion of Hungary, many in the PCF, particularly among the intellectuals, abandoned their allegiance to a communism which was becoming a powerful travesty of their hopes. In the post-war period, Éluard was particularly dependent after Nusch's death on strong, personal emotional ties with people in the PCF, especially Else Triolet and Louis Aragon. The latter became very influential in the PCF and was resolutely pro-Soviet, pro-Stalin. Éluard became emotionally entrenched against any open acknowledgement of signs of repression in the Soviet sphere of influence, though his poetry resonates with shadows of this. While some of his poems of this period returned time and again to an implicit landscape of loss of faith, bitterness and disillusionment, others articulated explicit faith in and dedication to a future invested in communism and, by association, Stalin, the USSR and its Eastern allies. Interestingly enough, these poems often used the most bland and prosaic language to be found in all of Éluard's work.

December 1950 saw publication of *Hommages / Tributes*, including its direct tributes to 'Joseph Staline' and 'L'URSS seule promesse'/'The USSR – the only promise', which Dominique insists he wrote on his own initiative without any Party pressure. These and other occasional poems of similar genre, though only a tiny percentage of his writing even in the last ten years of his life, have had an exaggerated influence on certain biases in later critical responses to Éluard's work. They have been invoked to support a condemnation of Éluard the communist, where his 'Stalinism' is read as sabotaging and contaminating his poetic project. This approach has informed one 'stock', oversimplified interpretation of his poetry which threatens to prevail now, with the collapse of communist regimes in the East and the even greater information available about the Stalinist era and its heritage. To illustrate this problematically partisan way of reading Éluard, it is worth mentioning the 1982 exhibition *Éluard et ses amis peintres / Éluard and his painter friends* at the Centre Pompidou in Paris. The largest exhibition ever mounted on Éluard's work, it displayed alongside Éluard's texts a highly visual exhibit of paintings, illustrations and photographs connected to his life and work-related collaborations. However, this visual density petered out rapidly into a stark, sparse selection of items from the moment the visitor passed Éluard's 1942 Communist Party re-enrolment card, enshrined alongside a book open at his poem to Stalin. These were both located near a recess in the exhibition hall, where non-stop recordings of hollow, resonant applause framed flags of Picasso's dove/face drawings from his and Éluard's 1951 *Le Visage de la Paix / The Face of Peace* (suggestiing of USSR-backed World Peace Congresses the two attended as prominent communist artists). Yet the last ten years of Éluard's writing produced poetic texts of the most diverse kind, covering over seven hundred pages in Volume II of the Pléiade edition of his complete works. These poems and poetic explorations are often connected implicitly to different dimensions of the Surrealist project, to the most diverse considerations of the political traditions of writing, and a multi-faceted concern with the processes of representation itself. This decade was deliberately edited out of the exhibition by the organisers, yet it involved some thirty works by Éluard produced in collaboration with visual artists. A homogenising and categorical anti-communism thus misses, or at best, under-represents a richly creative period of the poet's work, from which the collection presented here emerges.

One could perhaps keep in mind, even as one sifts through the complexities of the post-war political landscape in France, and the compromises, choices and priorities individuals made, these comments by Dominique, when in the 1980s she thought back on the last years of Éluard's life and his relationship to communism:

> In fact, for him the communist landscape was not at all a constrictive one...He did not know things which only became clear to people later. It was a kind of basis for his life, a central backcloth, to put it simply... He lived with a communist conscience, which was for him a form of generosity and fraternity.

She felt convinced that the revelations following Stalin's death would have been 'horrifying, even suicidal...very, very brutal' for Éluard and probably impossible for him to reconcile with Party membership.

Internal dilemmas and poetic affirmations: the Dominique years

During 1951 and 1952 Paul and Dominique had an apartment in Paris beside the Bois de Vincennes, but spent much of their time in Sarlat in the Périgord region. This was where Dominique originally came from, and where her mother still lived. Éluard found the Sarlat house very conducive to writing. They also spent a lot of time near Picasso in the South of France, where Dominique had an apartment in St Tropez. They were married there in June 1951, with Picasso and Françoise Gilot as witnesses, and celebrated the occasion with them and with Roland Penrose and his family at Picasso's house. That summer they met up with Tristan Tzara at Antibes.

In early 1951 Éluard brought out a new book of poetry, *Pouvoir tout dire / Able to Say Everything*, illustrated by Françoise Gilot. This opened with the poem 'Tout dire'/'To say everything' which returned structurally to the tense, ambivalent juxtaposition of doubt and willed confidence of *A Lesson in Morals*, which had preceded the 'over-clear', apparently unambivalent *Tributes*. Here he writes:

> What matters is to say everything but I lack the words
> I lack time and I lack daring
> I dream and reel-off haphazard images
> I have lived badly and failed to learn to speak clearly

Even love resonates in its complexity:

> Will I be able to express love its reasons
> Its leaden tragedy straw comedy
> Its daily repetitive acts
> And its immortalising caresses...
> ...Will I be able to compare need with desire
> And mechanical laws with laws of pleasure

Life, writing, love and politics are all framed here in a sense of paralysis, of a fear of inadequacy and failure and in open-ended questions which urgently underpin Éluard's poetic project: 'Will I have enough words to liquidate hate...Will I know how to colour the word revolution'. His *Response to a Questionnaire*, written at this time and circulated at a Venice writers' conference on the relationship of art to politics, stressed, however, his ascendant philosophy to work against the limits, the doubts, the inevitable compromises of entering into the actual contexts of the world:

> It is precisely from being daily at odds with what surrounds him that the artist finds the strength to create. He dreams of achieving and enabling that 'fundamental harmony' the world denies...Famine makes men want hunger to end, war makes them condemn murder, and injustice stirs in us a passion for justice. The artist is witness time and again, his role is as much to depict reality as it is to denounce crimes committed in its name...There is a crisis in contemporary art when... the artist allies himself too passively with a cruel, lying, damnable society...To know if an artist has fulfilled his mission well, criticism must first take into consideration all the conditions of his life, of things around him, of the place, the means, motives, mode of the time...The artist should reject wrong and give birth to what is good, his work should denounce and defy injustice, so that justice can become daily and tangible... If art is to be true, if it is to be a song of witness and a means

to action, it recognises that no reality, however horrifying, is overwhelming...The only quality we can demand from a creative artist is never to lack love, never to lack trust in human potential.

This belief in human potential framed the anthology Éluard published in the autumn of 1951, entitled *Première anthologie vivante de la poésie du passé / First Living Anthology of Poetry from the Past.* Here he assembled texts by writers from the twelfth to the seventeeth centuries, in a personal compilation of 'poets for whom tradition is invention and discovery', whose work Éluard saw as 'subversive in the name of morality' – a morality where the poet's project is 'to keep eyes open on oneself and on the world, on both sides of the mirror, to hold darkness at bay'. Here, once again, he moved in and out of the literary canon selectively, claiming a cultural landscape with no borders, seeking diversity and contrast, and including folklore, anonymous poems, neglected and forgotten writers. He set them alongside unexpected selections from the works of poets enshrined in tradition, favouring poems which evoked the power of images both to trace and to generate the human capacity for transformation.

At the same time as he brought into circulation the texts of former poets with whom he sensed an affinity, two powerful works of his own came into print in the same year. With Picasso, he produced *Le Visage de la Paix / The Face of Peace*, a work comprising twenty-nine short stanzas by Éluard juxtaposed by twenty-nine of Picasso's drawings, each combining a dove with a woman's face. The fluidity and lightness of the drawings echoed the simple, ascendant movement of Éluard's stanzas, leaning vividly into images of the human ability to claim peace, to side with life and envisage constructive forms of connection:

> Having washed his face in the sun
> Man needs to live
> Needs to let live and he gathers love
> Gathers the future   (stanza 17)
>
> Our songs call for peace
> And our replies are acts for peace   (stanza 24)
>
> The architecture of peace
> Rests on the whole world   (stanza 26)
>
> Open your wings lovely face
> Make the world behave
> For we are becoming real   (stanza 27)

44

It is not the shipwreck but our desire
That is irresistible and peace that is inevitable   (stanza 25)

We are becoming real together in our effort
Our will to dissolve shadows
On the dazzling path of new light   (stanza 28)

Picasso's dove emerged in these years as a powerful symbol for peace movements throughout the world in the second half of this century (one of the drawings from this collection would be used by the UK Campaign for Nuclear Disarmament in the 1980s). Éluard himself was virulently opposed to nuclear weapons. The collaboration on this small, inspirational work came out of the political terrain their close friendship was crossing in the early fifties. It captured the post-war imperative to contest the Cold War escalation of militarism – even as their communist affiliation held them contradictorily within the sphere of the Soviet arms build-up. His work moving on different levels again, Éluard also published a children's story *Grain-d'aile / Wing-seed*, a 'moral' tale of a girl dreaming to be a bird, only to re-enter her human form all the more gladly after seeing the constraints on a bird's existence. The story was illustrated by Jacqueline Duhème, a young woman whom Éluard became acquainted with by correspondence.

Le Phénix / The Phoenix, illustrated by Valentine Hugo, was also published in 1951. With its title image of the mythological bird, it marked permanent rebirth and the renewal of desire. The poems in this collection seem to assemble the poetic subjectivity of the lover through the self-evaluating processes of love. This process was now founded for Éluard in his relationship with Dominique. Her portrait introduced the collection. The title poem, contained under the regenerative sign of the phoenix, posited realism and hope ('mud and dew') as intrinsic to the love process. The desire to chart the complexity of factors involved in the self encountering another, and not to submerge that in romantic or sentimental simplifications, is at the heart of this work. It evokes the sense of passionate connection and intimate trust allowing the self to re-constitute wider desires, to give sense to a wider project where the couple is in movement in a social world. The 'woman' who figures in the poems under the feminine pronouns, under the referent sign of Dominique, does not move compliant to projections of the poet's desires, but while her 'warm flesh merges with (his) unleashed desires', contests, brings him down to earth, 'makes the sky fall onto the table'. The poet celebrates the challenge of her presence, the wide range of feelings – calmness or agitation – she evokes, and gives voice to his sense of enablement as he listens to her, is glad as he acknowledges the terms of her autonomous past. Images of feminine sweetness, youth and innocence are tempered with this female figure's association with resilience:

> ...stronger than thought
> Struggling to exist
> Firmer than life

He does not see her idealised by his projections, but acknowledges her weaknesses, her contestations, her autonomous 'wisdom different from mine', set 'against all forms of illusion', even as illusion forms an intrinsic element of the desire and pleasure experienced with her that the poems stage. The work is a fine tribute to the Dominique who would describe herself later in this way:

> ...feminist beliefs were influential to me all my life, as were communist ideas, though I was never a member of the Party...I always valued my autonomy and freedom and have always been so independent in my relationships with men that dominance was never an issue.

Éluard spoke on 'occasional poetry' in Geneva in February 1952, before travelling to Moscow as French representative for the Soviet celebrations of the 150th anniversary of the birth of Victor Hugo. In 1952 his collaboration with Elsa Triolet resulted in her biographical introduction to Éluard's adaptions of poems by the nineteenth-century Bulgarian socialist Christo Botev. The first volume of Éluard's three part *Anthologie des écrits sur l'art / Anthology of Writings on Art* appeared (the other two would come out posthumously). Here a diverse array of reproductions of art were offset by passages by art critics, writers and artists themselves. The volumes aimed to present texts and images which, Éluard wrote, 'best affirm the relationships that sight and art create between the world and man, man and society', which 'emphasise that physical light must inevitably have a corollary of moral light', which reveal 'the promethean passion which rivets the artist to his work' and which trace the hope and action which reconcile reality with the imagination. He reiterated his phrases from the 1930s, asserting:

> To see, is to understand and to act; seeing is about uniting the world to man and men to each other...To see, is to understand and love, to participate, commit oneself, judge, construct and know oneself within the scale of men and of the world.

He sought to present, he claimed, a wide diversity of personally chosen texts and images which were, in however diverse ways, immersed in desire for renewal, and which consciously or unconsciously contested 'the lie of art for art's sake'.

He spent the summer that year with Dominique and Caroline in the Dordogne, where he completed the manuscript of *Unbroken Poetry II* and prepared for publication a new anthology of his own poems, entitled *Poèmes pour tous: Choix de poèmes 1917-1952 / Poems for All: Selected Poems 1917-1952*. In this volume he chose to prioritise poems which invoked, from within different, either politically circumstantial or intimate journeys, the multi-faceted political agendas of his poetic trajectory. In early September, however, he suddenly suffered a stroke and was moved urgently to Paris for treatment and intensive rest. By early November he felt better, but wrote to his mother that he could not throw off a sense of overwhelming fatigue. He died suddenly from a further stroke on 18 November. The request for a state funeral was rejected by the government, but the streets of Paris were packed with thousands and thousands of people who gathered to pay their last respects to a passionately loved poet, en route to his burial at the Père Lachaise cemetery. In the next issue of *Les Lettres françaises* Picasso dedicated in memoriam to Éluard his drawing of a dove rising into flight.

Dominique has kept his name, through hers, in political circulation over the years since his death. For example, within a few years of Éluard's death her name stood beside Michel Foucault's at the forefront of the *Manifeste des 121*, a public manifesto supporting Algerian Independence and virulently opposing the French government's attempts to suppress the Algerian liberation movement. The signatories of this manifesto risked strong government reprisals over this, as French nationalist feeling about the war and about French military interventions in Algeria was running very high in France at the time. Dominique became actively involved for many years in *Les Droits des Détenus*, a human rights organisation campaigning for prisoners' rights, and she lent strong support to Central American solidarity struggles against political repression, especially in Guatemala. She set Éluard's voice to work for the feminist organisation *Choisir*, led by the socialist feminist lawyer Gisèle Halimi and supported by Simone de Beauvoir, which successfully fought through the liberalising reform of the abortion laws in France. *Choisir* carried banners with the photo of Picasso's plate illustrating the last stanza of Éluard's 'Castle of the Poor', from this collection, at the first national French Reproductive Rights women's demonstration in Paris in 1979. And recently Dominique has been a centrally active voice in anti-fascist, anti-

Le Pen initiatives in France. As muse to his inspiration, she has kept the name Éluard in political circulation in France in ways which have paid tribute to her political partner, to the voice in the 'Epitaphs' of *Unbroken Poetry II*:

> I am in your every day as the light is there
> Like a living man who is only warm on earth
>
> Only my hope and courage have remained
> You utter my name and you breathe more freely
>
> I had believed in you we are bountiful
> We go our way and happiness burns the past
>
> And our strength grows younger for all to see.

Unbroken Poetry II

Unbroken Poetry II is the last volume of poetry Éluard assembled. It appeared in February 1953, headed by a portrait of Éluard dedicated by Picasso to Dominique. Many of the poems had been individually published in journals, or were about to appear when Éluard died.

Unbroken Poetry II resumes themes Éluard came to see over the years as pivotal to his poetic practice. The last years of his work saw him in dialogue with the voices of many other poets, writers and artists, drawing out elements of their thought which resonated with his own, placing his own concerns within a larger cultural landscape of political agendas. In the same way, he was also in dialogue during these years with his own earlier works, re-framing them for republication, selecting, reorganising them and, in this case, continuing them, resuming the terms of poetic intervention which he saw as potentially unlimited. He explicitly linked this volume, by its title, to his 1946 *Unbroken Poetry*, suggesting how the poetic work exists not in its isolated artistic completion, but within continuing modulations of the poet's voice. Both volumes of *Unbroken Poetry* stage the processes of desire as central to a larger, social intervention which Éluard believed the love relationship could be imagined as galvanising, if love were rescripted and moved away from self-contained individualism towards a more socially conscious landscape.

Although at moments a density of syntax and fast juxtaposition of images and adjectives (which the English language is sometimes unable to follow) undermine any accessible narrative in these poems, Éluard's use of language here aims most often at familiarity of tone and syntax. The language tends towards simplicity of vision, for clarity in expressing the issues at stake, even as it charts the unresolved tensions of the self in the world and the self in relation to others. He saw his 'Epitaphs', which he wrote before any sign of his own ill-health, as working with a traditional convention for leaving behind, after death, traces of 'confidence and hope' to inspire the life of those who followed. And the epitaphs he wrote catch the flavour of the whole volume as they present images of movement into light and affirmation in the face of life's complicated, dark conditions:

> My heart suffered the wrongs
> Of injustice and unhappiness
> I lived in an unclean time...
>
> But in my nights I dreamed only of the blue sky...
>
> ...For my hope's sake I set my face against the dark

'Tarnished Emblems of my Dreams', apparently an unfinished text, powerfully evokes a sense of claustrophobic impossibility, subjective paralysis, horrifying airlessness, the absence of light or space, the traumatic loss of terms of reference for self-definition. Set within nightmare images, the text attempts to solve the human dilemma by escaping to a non-human animal world, where the poetic subject rises through processes of evolution only to find a new claustrophobia in a world reproduced merely for its own sake, devoid of consciousness or agency. These are all motifs at the heart of Éluard's landscape. He evokes a place of non-connection, non-communication and isolated passivity. It is the place where things merge mindlessly, nothing matters more than anything else, nothing differentiates the important from the irrelevant. It is a place of stifling stagnation, where the self is excluded from the possibility of choices, the options of self-positioning, where there is relentless persistence of the old order of things, with no possibility of change, only 'dregs of stillness', 'the same absolute chasm...the same place empty of image'. Here is where the poet mourns for himself, for the impossibility of his project, where all is inconsequential, all potential neutralised. It is the place of no language, of no communication, no moral vision, a consciousness only of impossibility, the antithesis of poetry itself. Roused from the nightmare, the poem in the end suggests a renewal of possibility though images of air, light, movement, connection and effort, as the sense of what it means to be human is given perspective by the negativities of the dream.

This dynamic – of charting what is not tenable, before repositioning both the poetic subject and the reader – shapes all the texts in this volume. It is a writing strategy of 'before and after', the significance of 'this' when set in contrast to 'that'. Éluard used it in many of his poems and works (e.g. *A Lesson in Morals*) especially after Nusch's death in 1946. It establishes a dialectical momentum within the texts, and generates a sense of movement within which the reader positions him/herself in relation to the options Éluard evokes. In 'It Is Not the Hands of Giants', emotional bankruptcy and disabled hope are nourished by self-centred individualism and counterpoint the urgent need for a collaborative social project. They prepare the scene for the 'we' whose task is to make human life significant and create the conditions for human happiness.

The two longer poems, 'Here There and Everywhere' and 'Castle of the Poor', have an unfinished, unfinishable feel to them. They end in full movement with no edge of structural completion to them. There is a sense, even, that they could have continued and ended later or never, since the poems insist on the permanent dialectical movement between the poet's anxieties and hopes. This dialectic operates between the poet's sense of possibility beyond the constraints of realism, between his reappraisal of the conditions to be faced and processes of interpretation that stretch desire and the frame of the couple. The poems are not there to resolve these tensions but present them as essential to a dynamic able to galvanise political involvement. The processes he wants to invoke are abstract, deployed in imaginary settings, but rooted in concrete references, in a staging of 'real' objects, landscapes, social processes and 'the couple'. These resonate for the reader as symptomatic of the emotional, political and social morality Éluard wants to inspire.

'Here There and Everywhere' deploys a strategy of contrasts to highlight the consequences of the use of language itself. It is a text about temporal, spatial and moral remapping, privileging the significance of effort and energy to engage in this process. It argues for the necessity of endlessly new departures, for paths of enablement. The poetic subject, even as it insists optimistically on possibilities of renewal, moves between this hope and sober reassessments of the forces at play which affect the possibility of departure. Language itself is the site in which transformation is possible, marking the responsibility of the writer for the consequences of what the writing selects, and for the agenda it elaborates. From a point where Éluard ponders on the way language constitutes the self through habits of representation and the conventions of ideological discourses, the poem goes on to exemplify the power of words to colour and to inform emotional vision. In long sections, which echo each other, a series of familiar concrete nouns (house, window, water, hand, table, bed, tiles, flower, sail, creeper, pearl, honey, etc) are first angled into a negative field of adjectives and verbs. There, 'turning away from desire', they lock the reader into images and feelings of disablement, closure, damage, constriction, sterility, wounding, thwarted possibilty and impotence. The language itself inhibits any movement of possibility through its powerfully negative framing of the nouns. The second section conjures up the same concrete nouns, but rescripts the words to form an affirmative field of renewal, with imagery of illumination, revival, enablement, collaboration, warmth, light. Éluard demonstrates in this process how choices shape meanings, with consequences that implicate the subject and object of the enunciation. Here and in 'Castle of the Poor', he gives a central place to his life-long belief in the enabling power of love in the energy of desire. Once again, loving acts as a pivot in moves towards valuing communication and promoting human welfare.

Where the 'you' enters the poem, the 'I' literally takes heart. The possibility of trust, touch, the 'passing on of fire', the exchange, the ecstasy of moments between lovers the need to create terms of justice and freedom where such possibilities can take shape for all, at different levels of personal want and social need. Images of war, militarism, colonialism, crippling social conditions and inhumanity haunt the edges of these two long poems. They repeatedly revert to re-examination of the conditions, of the accumulated experiences and the lived terms that impede and curtail new possibilities. The self is now burdened by a lack of grasp and direction, now caught in a sense of the futility of words, now gasping in a hot air of elusive idealism which edits out reality and blurs memory. But each time, from the sense of a compromised, flawed, inadequate grasp on the world, Éluard's text swings away from these compound negativities. Its ascendant energy is directed into an effort to make language a site of promise and potential, of invitation to move beyond how things are now, to rescript the world. The poetic project is to keep seeding an emotional terrain where new maps can be imagined, where a reality can emerge that responds to the associations of the poet's desire. 'What I love shall live' he writes, and the heart, the 'panoramic heart', is a place of survey, from where all must be reviewed, from where all will be desired, from where motivation will meet courage. The well-being of the lovers is fundamentally connected to their sense of agency in affecting conditions they inhabit.

51

Unbroken Poetry II is a text framed by Éluard's relationship with Dominique, and it is perhaps appropriate in the introduction to a love poet to end with some thoughts about the way the loved woman is constituted within these poems. Both 'Here There and Everywhere' and 'Castle of the Poor' trace histories of assimilation into passivity, impotence and complicity. The moments in the poems where the text breaks with old terms invoke a direct turning towards the presence of the loved woman. She may well be girl to his manhood here, child to his mastery there, protected and guided by his confidence in speaking. She may function to consolidate him, alert him by her differently gendered presence. To her he can speak himself; by her will he can be witnessed; he can herald in her access to speech by means of his own. But the invitation is nonetheless to a joint project, an exchange of well-wishing, an elaboration of a happiness which can navigate its mutual terms. A non-hierarchical solidarity is at stake. She is constituted through contrasting possibilities, where her agenda prevails even as she meets him. If she is 'ravenous', she is 'satiated' too; she is loved both 'sour' and 'ripe', in her own seasonal growth, not necessarily accommodated to him. She is as well 'loved' as she is well 'loving', active and passive, daring to ride the storm on her own terms, even as she accompanies his images of health, his passion for life. He wants to harvest with her their future, not just his; he wants them both

> to go beyond
> All that we were

If the 'us' is originally constituted as part of the problem, new counter-texts of a rescripted 'us' now constitute possibilities of solution. Conventions must be moved, metamorphoses imagined and enacted. She stands for impatience, impetuous intervention, courage. Their journey opens up a critical charting of the bastions of power which damage, revealing the invisible ideological structures which cement forms of normative legitimacy in human interaction. 'Castle of the Poor' names Dominique as distinctly positioned, signposting the hopes of new trajectories infused with processes of enablement. With nuanced poignancy and tenderness, the masculine subject invokes the feminine object of desire, calling on her to listen to him – not to witness his potency, his mastery, nor to follow his agenda, but to witness his contradictions, his dependency on her, his points of despair and exhaustion, his complicity with the problems he seeks to solve, his frequent sense of loss of potency, the struggles he moves through to find his footing on those ascendant paths of hope and affirmation to which he is so crucially commited. His process, his efforts, his dilemmas, his hopes are opened to her by the text itself. As he must strive to put into words all that must be said, she shall witness it all. She is part of the recognition of the significance of the journey being attempted, even as she forges and travels its path with him. The poem is in conversation with her, urged on by her, urging her in turn. She is implicated because she is there, because they move on in relation to each other, because their connection makes dialogue possible and sets things in motion.

Though language renders the project larger than the particular, the directness of address, the tenderness of intimacy, the pleasure of being in the presence of each other are suggestive of a highly particularised letter, weaving the fruits of ongoing dialogues onto the sparseness of the poetic page. Perhaps having traced for Éluard's anglophone readers the paths of politicial engagements his poetry leans on, the political agendas which persistently inform the emotional tenor of his writing and the deeply political life which nourished his poetic practice, it is time to stand back from that narrative and return the text you are about to read to its personal context. And let Éluard's love tribute to the Dominique his texts encapsulate stand with its particular flavour, its highly specific processes, its struggles and celebration. For if politics inform the project, those politics imply recognition of personal processes in specific relationships. Their particular interventions in the difficult hierarchies of power lie right at the quick of loving and the desires for social transformation that loving may sustain. That specificity is named here in this text, as it was incorporated into *The Phoenix* when Éluard wrote, with a phrase inscribing Dominique Éluard in anagrammatic form ('dora d'unique miel'):

> The hive of your flesh under the singular sun
> Coats with singular honey my awakening sky

and caught the emotional angle of his desire for her in that liberatory conjuncture his poetic creativity persistently affirmed, against all odds:

> I love you I can feel in my very bones
> Emancipation from shadows

Selected Bibliography

PAUL ÉLUARD: Major works

Oeuvres complètes, Volumes I & II, edited by Marcelle Dumas and Lucien Scheler (Paris: Gallimard, Bibliothèque de la Pléïade, 1968). This is a key source to all Éluard's poetry and prose writing and includes also many of the manifestos and collective texts he signed. Annotated edition, with a comprehensive bibliography giving publication details of individual works by Éluard up to 1968. Éluard was, particularly after the war, an extremely popular poet, with many of his works frequently individually available in print.

Lettres de Jeunesse, presented by Cécile Valette-Éluard and Robert D. Valette (Paris: Seghers, 1962).

Éluard, livre d'identité, edited by Robert D. Valette (Vevey: Tchou, 1967).

Paul Éluard: le poète et son ombre, edited by Robert D. Valette (Paris: Seghers, 1963). These volumes assemble photographs, letters, drawing, postcards, tracing aspects of Éluard's life, relationships, collaborations, daily life and social and political connections.

Lettres à Gala (1924-1948) (Paris: NRF, Gallimard, 1984); English version translated by Jesse Browner (New York: Paragon House, 1989).

Anthologie des écrits sur l'art (Paris: Éditions Cercle d'Art), vols. I-III, 1972).

PAUL ÉLUARD: English Translations

Thorns of Thunder: Selected Poems, edited by George Reavey, translation by Samuel Beckett et al (London: Europa Press & S. Nott, 1936).

Paul Éluard: Selected Poems, selected and translated by Gilbert Bowen, introduced by Max Adereth (London: Calder, 1987).

The Immaculate Conception, Paul Éluard and André Breton, translated by John Graham (London: Atlas, 1990).

Ombres et soleil / Shadows and Sun: Selected writings of 1913-1952, translated by Lloyd Alexander & Cicely Buckley (Durham, NH: Oyster River Press, 1995).

PAUL ÉLUARD: Further Reading

BOOKS:

Daniel Berguez: *Éluard ou le rayonnement de l'être* (Seyssel: Éditions du Champ Vallon, 1982).

Jean-Yves Debreuille: *Éluard ou le pouvoir du mot: Propositions pour une lecture* (Paris: Nizet, 1977).

Luc Decaunes: *Paul Éluard: L'amour, la révolte, le rêve* (Paris: Balland, 1982).

J.-C. Gateau: *Paul Éluard et la peinture surréaliste 1910-1939* (Geneva: Droz, 1982).

J.-C. Gateau: *Éluard, Picasso et la peinture 1936-1952* (Geneva: Droz, 1982).

Puntus Hulton (ed.): *The Surrealists Look at Art: Éluard, Aragon, Soupault, Breton, Tzara*, translated by Michael Palmer et al (Venice: Lapis Press, 1990).

Ursula Jucker-Wehrli: *La poésie de Paul Éluard et le thème de la pureté* (Zurich: Juris-Verlag, 1965).

J.P. Juillard: *Le regard dans la poésie d'Éluard* (La Pensée Universelle, 1972).

Atle Kittang: *D'amour de poésie: essai sur l'univers des metamorphoses dans l'œuvre surréaliste de Paul Éluard* (Paris: Minard, Lettres Modernes, 1969).

Maryvonne Meuraud: *L'image végétale dans la poésie d'Éluard* (Paris: Minard, Lettres Modernes, 1966).

Raoul Pantanella: *L'amour et l'engagement d'après l'oeuvre de Paul Éluard* (Travaux et Mémoires XXII, La Pensée Universitaire, Faculté des Lettres d'Aix-en-Provence, 1962).

Louis Parrot: *Paul Éluard* (Paris: Seghers, 1953).

Centre Georges Pompidou: *Paul Éluard et ses amis peintres* (catalogue to exhibition of the same title, Paris, 1982).

Louis Perche: *Paul Éluard* (Paris: Éditions Universitaires, 1963).

Jean Raymond: *Paul Éluard par lui-même* (Paris: Écrivains de toujours, Seuil, 1968).

Roger-Jean Ségalat: *Album Éluard*, third volume of *Oeuvres complètes*: on Éluard's life and work (Paris: Gallimard, Bibliothèque de la Pléiade, 1968).

Richard Vernier: *Poésie ininterrompue et la poétique de Paul Éluard* (Paris & The Hague: Mouton, 1971).

ARTICLES & CHAPTERS:

Sonia Assa: 'Hairdressers and Kings: Ready-made Revelations in *Les Malheurs des Immortels*', in *French Review*, Champaign, Il, (March 1991), 64:4, 643-58.

Mary Ann Caws: 'Paul Éluard' in *The Poetry of Dada and Surrealism* (Princeton University Press, 1970).

Peter Collier: 'The Poetry of Protest: Auden, Aragon and Éluard' in P. Collier & E. Timms (eds.), *Visions and Blueprints: Avant-garde Culture and Radical Politics in Early 20th Century Europe* (Manchester University Press, 1988).

Stephen Walton: 'Parody and poetry in Éluard's Proverbs', in *Romance Languages Annual*, West Lafayette, Indiana (1992), 4, 166-70.

AILLEURS ICI PARTOUT
HERE THERE EVERYWHERE

...Il y a quelque adresse à avoir mis mes idées dans la bouche d'un homme qui rêve: il faut souvent donner à la sagesse l'air de la folie, afin de lui procurer ses entrées; j'aime mieux qu'on dise: «Mais cela n'est pas si insensé qu'on croirait bien», que de dire: «Écoutez- moi, voici des choses très-sages.»

DIDEROT
Lettres à Sophie Volland

Là se dressent les mille murs
De nos maisons vieillissant bien
Et mères de mille maisons
Là dorment des vagues de tuiles
Renouvelées par le soleil
Et portant l'ombre des oiseaux
Comme l'eau porte les poissons

Là tous les travaux sont faciles
Et l'objet caresse la main
La main ne connaît que promesses
La vie éveille tous les yeux
Le corps à des fièvres heureuses
Nommées la Perle de midi
Ou la Rumeur de la lumière

Là je vois de près et de loin
Là je m'élance dans l'espace
Le jour la nuit sont mes tremplins
Là je reviens au monde entier
Pour rebondir vers chaque chose
Vers chaque instant et vers toujours
Et je retrouve mes semblables

Je parle d'un temps délivré
Des fossoyeurs de la raison
Je parle de la liberté
Qui finira par nous convaincre
Nul n'aura peur du lendemain
L'espoir ne fait pas de poussière
Rien ne sera jamais en vain

Here rise the thousand walls
Of our houses ageing now
And here are mothers from a thousand houses
Here sleep ripples of tiles
Made new by the sun
They bear along the shadow of birds
As water bears the shadow of fish

Here all tasks come easily
What is to be done fondles the hand
Promises are all the hand knows
Life opens every eye from sleep
The body has gladsome fevers
Called the Pearl of the middle day
Or the Clamour of the light

Here I see near and far
Here I hurl myself into space
Day and night are places where I leap
Here I return to the whole world
To rebound on anything I choose
At any moment that I choose
And I discover my fellow creatures

I speak of a time made free
Of the grave-diggers of reason
I speak of freedom
Which finally will prove
How none shall fear the morrow
Hope raises no dust
Nothing shall ever be in vain

Je cherche à me créer une épreuve plus dure
Qu'imaginer ce monde tel qu'il pourrait être
Je voudrais m'assurer du concret dans le temps
Partir d'ici et de partout pour tout ailleurs

Ouvrir vraiment à l'homme une porte plus grande

Il faut reprendre le langage en son milieu
Équilibrer l'écho la question la réponse
Et que l'image transparente se reflète
En un point confluent cœur du panorama

Cœur du sang et du sens et de la conscience

Voici ma table et mon papier je pars d'ici
Et je suis d'un seul bond dans la foule des hommes
Mes mots sont fraternels mais je les veux mêlés
Aux éléments à l'origine au souffle pur

Je veux sentir monter l'épi de l'univers

J'ai le sublime instinct de la pluie et du feu
J'ensemence la terre et rends à la lumière
Le lait de ses années fertiles en miracles
Et je dévore et je nourris l'éclat du ciel

Et je ne crains que l'ombre atroce du silence

Je prononce la pierre et l'herbe y fait son nid
Et la vie s'y reflète excessive et mobile
Le duvet d'un aiglon mousse sur du granit
Une faible liane mange un mur de pierres

Le chant d'un rossignol amenuise la nuit

Prise d'en haut d'en bas dans ma voix fléchissante
La forêt s'agglutine ou se met en vacances
Ravines et marais dans ma voix renaissante
S'allègent comme un corps qui se dévêt et chante

Mers et plaines déserts le jour naît sur la terre

I shall try to devise a harsher test
Than imagining this world as it might be
I mean to make sure about the real here and now
Begin from here and there and everywhere

And open to man himself a wider door

We must restore men's speech where it belongs
Balance echo question answer
So that the revealing image is displayed
Where it meets the panorama's beating heart

Heart of blood of feeling and mind

This is my table my paper here I begin
And with one leap I am with the mass of men
My words are brotherly but I want them to blend
With the primeval with pure inspiration

I want to feel rise the eye of the universe

With proud instinct with rain and fire
I scatter seed on earth give back to light
The milk of its years so rich in miracles
And gaze upon the sky and feed its glare

And all I fear is the odious shadow of silence

I say this is stone and grass will nestle there
And life unfolds excessive and in motion
The down of an eaglet clusters on granite
A thin plant creeps and gnaws a wall of stone

The song of a nightingale diminishes the night

Held high and low in my relenting voice
The forest shapes into folds or seeks respite
Deeps and shallows in my reviving voice
Ease like a body that bares itself and sings

Over desert and plain and sea the day breaks over earth

Victorieux enjeu des couleurs des saveurs
La fleur est le ferment de ma langue bavarde
Le temps ne passe pas quand le bruit étincelle
Et refait chaque aurore en nommant une fleur

Ce monde je le veux éprouver sur mon cœur

Dans chaque cœur battant j'en entendrai l'écho
Un pas après un pas la route est infinie
L'animal a conduit ses gestes vers leur but
Et je me suis déduit de leur nécessité

Son sommeil a bordé le lit où je repose

De mort je ne sais rien sauf qu'elle est éphémère
Et je veux chaque soir coucher avec la vie
Et je veux chaque mort coucher avec la vie
L'hiver l'oubli n'annoncent que l'avenir vert

Je ne me suis jamais vu mort les hommes vivent

Je parle et l'on me parle et je connais l'espace
Et le temps qui sépare et qui joint toutes choses
Et je confonds les yeux et je confonds les roses
Je vois d'un seul tenant ce qui dure ou s'efface

La présence a pour moi les traits de ce que j'aime

C'est là tout mon secret ce que j'aime vivra
Ce que j'aime a toujours vécu dans l'unité
Les dangers et les deuils l'obscurité latente
N'ont jamais pu fausser mon désir enfantin

De tous les points de l'horizon j'aime qui m'aime

Je ne vois clair et je ne suis intelligible
Que si l'amour m'apporte le pollen d'autrui
Je m'enivre au soleil de la présence humaine
Je m'anime marée de tous ses éléments

Je suis créé je crée c'est le seul équilibre
C'est la seule justice

Triumph of colour and taste
The flower is the ferment of my chattering tongue
Time does not pass when the broken silence flickers
And proclaims each dawn with the name of a flower

This world I want to learn to know within my heart

In every heart beat I shall hear the echo
One step after another the road is infinite
The animal has marked its paces to an end in view
And I have walked away from what it needs

Its sleep enfolds me in the comfort where I rest

Of death I know nothing save its transience
And every night I shall lie down with life
At every death I shall lie down with life
Winter and neglect promise the future green

I have never thought of myself as dead because men live

I speak they speak to me I know infinity
And time that separates and joins all things
Roses and eyes I do confound
But all at once I see what lasts or fades

Presence for me has the stuff of what I love

It is there my secret what I love shall live
What I love has always lived as one
The dangers and the sorrows and the darkness hiding
Could never disappoint my childhood's desire

Along the range of view I love whatever loves me

I see clearly and I can be understood
Only if love will waft to me the dust of others
I revel in the sun of human presence
I quicken in the tide of all its parts

Created I create this is the only poise
The only justice

Entre chez moi toi ma santé
Entre chez moi toi ma passion de vivre
Ne doute plus de rien sois gaie
Car je veux te donner plus de raisons de rire
Que de pleurer entre chez moi ma bien-aimante
Viens m'éclairer

Entre chez moi toi mon tourment
Pour oublier notre chagrin
Entre chez moi vorace et rassasiée
Grain de raisin trop vert ou éclaté
Viens mon audace au large des orages
Viens amasser notre avenir

Vois-tu je dis chez moi et c'est déjà pour rire
Ce n'est qu'en moi que je veux dire
Ma force t'y reçoit ton image y prend corps
Je t'offre un toit je t'offre un lit plus grand que toi
J'y suis déjà couché dans la plaine et les bois
Et c'est le flot montant de la mer qui t'envoie

Entre en moi toi ma multitude
Puisque je suis à jamais ton miroir
Ma figurée
Les rues vont loin qui passent par nos villes
Loin dans les champs où l'on avance
Avec l'amour avec la vie avec le jour

Entre en moi toi toujours meilleure
Toujours semblable à mes désirs
Illimitée et torturée et rassurée
Toutes voiles tombées toutes voiles dehors
Creusée de nuit et de lumière
Et captant le silence et drainant la rumeur

Toi qui voulais une maison
Tu t'en délivres
Car la maison que je te donne
N'a sa façade ouverte qu'en exemple à tous
Notre maison n'est bonne que pour en sortir
Nous rêvons d'une autre maison au fond des âges

Enter in my house you my health
Enter in my house you my passion for living
Doubt nothing more be free of care
For I will give you cause for laughter
More than for tears enter in my house my loving one
Come to light my way

Enter in my house you my torment
So we forget our grief
Enter in my house devouring and replete
Grape too sour or overripe
Come my daring one that rides the storm
Come and build our future up

Look I say my house but that is just for fun
Come where I am is what I mean
My strength will welcome you your image will take shape
I give you a roof a bed more ample than you need
There I have lain under the sky and in the woods
It is the swell of the sea that sends you here

Come where I am you my multitude
I shall for ever be your looking glass
The proof of me in another guise
Streets through our towns go far
Far into fields through which we stride
With love with life all through the day

Come where I am I see you clearer
All the time the shape of my desires
Strained and unconfined and reassured
All sails lowered all sails set
You in the alleys of the night and light
Enticing the silence and draining the sound

You who sought a house
You are now free of care
For the house I give you with its open doors
Is just a warning to everyone
Our house is right only for departures
We dream of another house in the far beyond

Captifs d'un seul moment un moment nous délivre
Le temps des amoureux qui passeront le pont
Que nous avons passé avant de nous connaître
Les flots de l'avenir les séparent encore
Mais leur lèvre a la courbe d'un seul mot je t'aime
Leurs mains sont la promesse d'une main doublée

Entre en moi toi ma paresseuse ma berceuse
Je n'ai pas de secrets pour toi
Avec toi je n'ignore rien
Tu es faite pour tout savoir
Je te dis tout au tableau noir
De mon passé de ma jeunesse

Car tout n'a pas été si facile ni gai

Hier il y a très longtemps
Je suis né sans sortir des chaînes
Je suis né comme une défaite

Hier il n'y a pas longtemps
Je suis né dans les bras tremblants
D'une famille pauvre et tendre
Où l'on ne gagnait rien à naître

On parlait bas comprenait sourd
Ma famille est née de l'oubli
D'un peuple d'ombres sans reflets

Chaque jour les miens me fêtaient
Mais je n'étais à la mesure
Ni de moi-même ni des grands
Je n'avais pour but que l'enfance

Dans les méandres de ma chambre
Fermée aux jeux de l'impatience
Je ne rêvais que de fenêtres

Et je riais et je criais
À faire fondre le soleil
Mais je pleurais à faire rire
De mon chagrin la terre entière

Held in a single moment a moment that frees
The time for lovers who will cross the bridge
We crossed before we knew each other
The tides of the future still divide them
But their lips have the curve that says I love you
And their hands are the promise of hands joined together

Come where I am you my sleepy one my lullaby
I keep no secrets from you
With you I am aware of everything
You are made to know everything
I will tell you what the chronicle says
About my youth and past

For not everything was so easy or free of care

Yesterday a long time ago
I was born still clasped in chains
Birth was like a defeat

Yesterday not so long ago
I was born in the trembling arms
Of a poor and loving family
There was nothing to be gained by being born

We spoke softly understood in silence
My family was the issue of neglect
Children of shadows without reflection

Every day they made a fuss of me
But I could not come to terms
Either with them or with myself
Childhood was my only purpose

Pacing all around my room
Closed to the tricks of hastiness
I dreamed only of windows

And I used to laugh and cry aloud
Enough to melt the sun
Shed tears enough to make the whole world
Laugh about my sorrows

Et puis l'injure me fut faite
Je fus d'un seul coup déréglé
Les monstres prenaient pied sur moi

L'or sonnait mat et frappait lourd
On pêchait dans l'eau d'un diamant
De sales de lugubres bêtes
On assassinait les poètes

J'avais vingt ans et je faisais
Déjà la guerre pour nos maîtres
Ils avaient besoin de jeunesse

Je fus naïf au point de ne pas me défendre
Je recevais les coups sans songer à les rendre
J'étais fait comme tous de matière sensible
Les flammes me semblaient avoir l'azur pour cible

Dans ma candeur aux femmes je me déchirais
Aux fleurs je me fanais aux fruits je me gâtais
L'ordre de la nature embaumait mon supplice
Mais j'avais par à-coups de terribles colères

Et je voulais avoir des griffes pour en jouir
Contre les hommes et les femmes à genoux
Contre les hommes et les femmes en mal d'être
Contre l'enfant trop clair et contre ses désirs

D'astre en astre ma violence
A fait justice des vertus
Qui pourrissaient dans l'égoïsme
Ma tête s'est révélée nue
Je ne savais pas simuler
Ni figurer une statue
Qui ne soit pas dans tout l'espace

La verdure au gré de la mer
Et des forêts et de l'aurore
Au gré des vagues et des feuilles
Et de la minime lueur
Qui pénètre dans chaque cœur
Pour le confondre et l'augmenter
Dissipe la nuit et l'hiver

And then insult was done to me
All at once I was made mad
Monsters trampled over me

Gold rang flat struck dull
In the brilliance of a diamond
They looked for dark and ugly creatures
They murdered poets

I was twenty and already
Had gone to war for our masters
They needed youth

I was so simple I did not defend myself
I took blows I never dreamed of giving back
Like everyone I was made of sensitive stuff
Flames seemed to aim for the blue sky

In my artlessness with women I agonised
With flowers I withered with fruits I just indulged
The ways of nature sweetened my distress
Yet without warning I had terrible spells of rage

And I wanted claws to enjoy my anger
Against men and women on their knees
Against men and women in their want
Against the bright child and its wishes

From star to star my violence
Ended the myth of virtues
That rotted in selfishness
My way of thinking was exposed
I could not pretend to be
Nor look like any statue
Whose element is not the beyond

The greenness at the mercy of the sea
Of the forest and the break of day
At the mercy of the waves and leaves
And of the merest gleam
That finds its way into every heart
To confound and amplify it
And dispels the night and winter

Et d'évidence en évidence
Je parle en témoin éclairé
Et la trame me paraît douce
De ce que je couvre de vie
Le mal est vain et la mort vide
Douter est une comédie
Que l'on se joue pour mieux sauter

Et mon regard pourtant connaît la parenté
Et le monde déduit de ce qu'il fut toujours
Il prend feu sans détruire il a tous les mérites
Il entraîne la femme au delà de son rythme
Il entraîne l'enfant au delà du vieillard
En route les cailloux effeuillés sont les pierres
De la ville amassée où chacun a son frère

J'entends ce soir j'entends encore dans ma fièvre
Un cri réel d'enfant robuste et bienheureux
Une plainte de femme exquise et souveraine
Un appel d'homme au fond de la vérité même
Et je répète un rêve qui me vient de loin
Voir clair et parler clair régner dans l'éternel
Moi qui n'ai jamais pu m'assombrir qu'un instant

Je sais que si je dis le bien je veux le bien
Sur l'heure et pour toujours je dis je veux le miel
Et l'ondulation du miel comme des blés
Se propage à mon souffle et ses rides ardentes
M'accordent le pouvoir de ne rien abjurer
J'espère j'ai pu vaincre ma naissance obscure
Le fait de commencer n'est qu'une illusion

Le réel table
Sur le réel

Et la morale
Sur la morale

Je vis d'un bien nécessaire
Et d'un monde profitable

Je vis d'un élan constant
Arriver est un départ

And from the obvious to the obvious
I speak as a knowing witness
And the thread I weave over life
Seems gentle to me
Evil is vain and death empty
Doubting is make-believe
With which we frolic the better to leap

And yet my eyes know affinity
And the world is what it always was
It catches fire without destroying has its worth
It sweeps the woman beyond her rhythm
It sweeps the child beyond old age
On its way the scattered pebbles are the stones
Of the teeming city where everyone has a brother

This evening I hear I still hear in my fever
The natural cry of a strong and blessed child
The lament of a radiant and matchless woman
The call of a man from the depth of truth itself
And I repeat a dream returning from afar
Speaking and seeing clearly eternal peace
I who never knew sadness but for a moment

I know that if I speak of good I mean the good
Then and for always I say I want the honey
And the wafts of honey like the wafts of corn
Spread to my breath and my eager breath
Grants me the power nothing to retract
I hope and I have overcome obscure birth
The fact of beginning is only illusion

The real depends
On the real

And the moral
On the moral

I live by necessary blessings
And by a world that yields

I live by constant verve
To arrive is to depart

Vieillir c'est organiser
Sa jeunesse au cours des ans

C'est mûrir mille jeunesses
Par étés et par automnes

Tenir son vol assez haut
Pour que l'aile y ait un but

C'est ruiner l'ombre quotidienne
Sur des sommets perpétuels

C'est faire honneur à l'avenir

Je me répète à la mesure où je suis homme
Et je m'étonne que personne
N'ait pu valablement
Me démentir parler pour moi sans que résonne
Aussitôt plus pure ma voix
Et sans le vouloir j'ai raison
Sans le vouloir je suis de tous les temps

Les mots qui me sont interdits me sont obscurs
Mais les mots qui me sont permis que cachent-ils
Les noms concrets
D'où viennent-ils vers moi
Sur ce flot d'abstractions
Toujours le même
Qui me submerge

En moi si tout est mis au bien
Tout vient du mal et du malheur

Les mots comme les sentiments
Ce n'est pas pour rien qu'on hérite
De l'auréole des victimes
Des cauchemars du désespoir
Et de la haine et de l'angoisse
D'une foule vaincue et lasse
Tombée à la première marche

To grow old is to order
One's youth in the flow of years

It is to let bloom the thousand flowers of youth
Through summers and through autumns

To stay in flight so high
That wings have a destination

It is to blow away the dark of every day
Over the ageless mountain tops

It is to honour the future

This I repeat to myself for I am a man
And I am amazed that no one
Could with reason
Contradict me speak for me without my voice
Re-echoing most pure all at once
I do not wish it I am in the right
I do not wish it I belong to eternity

Words denied to me are hard to understand
But words allowed what do they conceal
Real names
From what beginning do they come upon me
On this unchanging
Torrent of abstractions
Flooding over me

If everything is done for the good in me
Then everything comes from the bad and the unhappy

Words like feelings
It is not for nothing we inherit
The glory of victims
The nightmares of despair
And the hate and anguish
Of a tired and conquered crowd
Fallen at the first step

Le mot maison dans leur ville les pauvres
Sont plus pauvres de leur maison

Le mot fenêtre un mur le bouche

Soleil les papillons s'entassent
Le désert s'infiltre partout

L'eau bouclier crevé d'avance

Les mains esclaves flammes vaines
Travaillent sans savoir pourquoi

Table verrou de l'appétit

Tuiles d'avoir vu rose sous l'azur bien sage
Un enfant se déprave au contact de la nuit

Et sa chair est en loques

Caresse laine sacrifiée
Chemin d'hiver et de vieillesse

Au gué de la rivière on oublie les infirmes

Le mot chambre bolide à jamais dans la boue
Éclatant ressort détendu

Souche calcinée et stérile

Marais bouquet marbré d'odeurs
Grille multipliée du plomb

Fleur fille épaisse des couleurs

Le lit étendard de défaite
Lumière fade verre vide

Le mot miroir où la beauté mendie son pain

Joli rossignol dans la nuit
Ouvre les plaies de l'insomnie

The word house in their cities the poor
Are poorer because of their houses

The word window a wall blocks it

Sun and butterflies crowd together
Everywhere the desert seeps

Water a shield already pierced

Slave hands vain flames
Work without knowing why

Table a bolt on appetite

Bad luck to have seen the rosy side under the lazy blue sky
A child is sinful on acquaintance with the night

And finds its flesh in shreds

An embrace is wool sacrificed
The road to winter and old age

At the ford over the river the weak are forgotten

The word room a thunderbolt fast in the mire
When it bursts a loosened spring

A stump charred and barren

Marsh a posy veined with odours
A grating laced with lead

Flower a girl dense with colour

Bed is a banner of defeat
Dull light empty glass

The word mirror where beauty begs for its bread

Pretty nightingale in the night
Opens the wounds of sleeplessness

Que la forêt soit ta charpie

Le mot porte cri d'agonie
Calcul pourri de l'évasion

La vague d'où l'on ne sort plus

Le sang d'un homme se répand
En moins d'une heure pour toujours

Le sang d'un homme fait horreur

Le sang d'un homme répond non
À toute question quand il meurt

Le mot tremplin surgit des reins de la vipère

Statue monstre d'indifférence
Battant arraché de la cloche

Panorama tout se ramène au plus petit

Le mot façade crépuscule
Pavé suivant l'ordre établi

Aiglon tremblant fils du vertige

Et les toits se couvrent de neige
Ou de chiendent comme des tombes

Les mains heureuses ont trahi

Elles n'ont rien trouvé de bon
Dans la nature ni dans l'homme

Dix doigts c'est trop peu pour comprendre

Pierre insensible puits massif
Où le squelette boit son ombre

Épi scolopendre immobile

Let the forest be your bandage

The word door is a cry of agony
Rotted motive of breaking free

The wave from which there is no escape

The blood of a man spills
In less than an hour and for always

The blood of a man horrifies

The blood of a man answers no
To any question when he dies

The word springboard leaps from the viper's back

A statue a monster of indifference
A clapper torn from the bell

Panorama everything reduced to its smallest

The look of things a decline
Built according to the rules

Trembling eaglet son of the great heights

And the roofs are blanketed with snow
Or with creeping grass like graves

Happy hands have played false

They have found nothing good
Neither in nature nor in man

Ten fingers are too few for understanding

Unfeeling stone is a massive well
Where the skeleton drinks its shadow

Ear of corn a motionless centipede

Lèvres les ailes d'un moulin
Qui tourne à rebours des désirs

Chaines faveurs autour des jambes

Le mot pollen comme un crachat
Comme un palais jeté par terre

Orage horloge détraquée

Dures perles séchant sur pied
Feu monnayable des vertus

Tous les yeux dans leur rouille crasse

Le mot marée porte la peste
La musique de l'ennemi

La griffe est un doigt juste sur un clavier faux

L'arbre s'abat le feu s'éteint
Le pont se brise comme un os

La liane se grave en cicatrice ignoble

Le miel encrasse amèrement la ruche morte
La voile j'ai connu qu'elle se couche et flotte

Ainsi j'ai perdu mon élan

Et les premières rides
Ont ficelé ma face

Et j'ai compris

À partir de la nuit
Je renverse le mal j'échafaude l'espoir
En montant sur des ruines

Lips are the sails of a windmill
Turning away from desire

Chains are favours around the legs

The word pollen like spittle
Like a palace razed to the ground

Storm a clock in disarray

Rough pearls going to waste
Fires that can be tamed by purity

All eyes in their mould

The word tide brings in the plague
The music of the enemy

A claw is the right finger on the wrong note

The tree crashes the fire dies down
The bridge cracks like a bone

The creeping plant leaves its mark in a hideous scar

The honey corrodes the dead hive
The sail I know that it folds and drifts

And so I lost my verve

And the first furrows
Sewed up my face

And I understood

From the night onwards
I overturn the wrong I build hope up
By climbing over the ruins

Qu'ai-je jamais pensé dans mon passé sinistre
Qui vaille le matin qui vaille le travail
D'une main courageuse au seuil de la confiance
Et j'apprends à tisser une dentelle d'ailes
Et de salutations à tout ce que je nomme
Pour les temps à venir

Une dentelle au point d'aurore
Crible d'yeux clairs et de claires paroles
Fini de fuir j'avance et je m'anime
De la sève d'un feu lucide
Je jure et mon serment ne peut jamais faillir
Que sinon moi les autres oublieront le mal

Ils seront maîtres d'eux-mêmes
Toujours à leur premier geste
Toujours à leur premier mot
Toujours sans défauts leurs rides
Auront la beauté de l'aube
Quand les yeux ont reposé

Il fallait que je dise tout ce que j'ai dit
Car je viens de moins loin qu'où mes frères iront
Et je veux me survivre

Je veux mourir et vivre par un mot sans bornes
Ce premier mot c'est toi
Toi telle que tu es inaugurant mon ordre

Toi qui joins tout ce qui est vrai
Ma bien-aimée ma bien-aimante
Semblable aux saisons sans regrets
Toi qui me permets d'échapper
À la facilité de vivre
Par des mensonges même au nom de la vertu

Même au nom de la vérité

La vérité c'est liberté
C'est la fleur et le fruit promis
C'est la fécondité par delà toute faim
Par delà toute cécité

What did I ever think in my forbidding past
What might the day be worth what worth the toil
Of a hand of courage where trust begins
And I learn to weave a pattern of wings
And greetings to everything I name
For the times to come

A pattern at the break of day
A web of sparkling eyes and lucid words
When flight is done I go my way I quicken
With the core of a blazing fire
I make my vow and my oath can never fail
Unless I fail the others will forget the evil done

They will be masters of what they do
From their very first step
From their very first word
With never a blemish their frowns
Shall have the beauty of the dawn
When eyes have rested

I needed to say all I have said
For I come from a nearer place than where my brothers go
And I want to stand the test of time

I want to die and live by a limitless word
That first word is you
You as you are who shadow forth the way I live

You who join together every truth
My beloved my loving one
Like the seasons without regrets
You who help me to break free
From the easy way of living
Even by deception in the name of virtue

Even in the name of truth

Truth is freedom
The blossom and the promised fruit
It is abundance beyond all hunger
Beyond all sightlessness

Statue il n'y a plus qu'une statue sur terre
Elle a le fier maintien de l'homme sur la terre

Un seul toit unit tous les ciels
Chaque maison n'est qu'un caprice

L'horizon borde mes paupières
Par quel miracle aurais-je peur

L'espace est le filet de lait
Qui me nourrit et m'éternise

Panorama j'absorbe au fond d'un puits profond
Le ciel plein jusqu'aux bords de reflets et d'étoiles

L'étoile augmente les étoiles
Nous savons marier les saisons

Nous savons défaire les nœuds
De ce qui n'est que contingences

Les vieilles neiges rajeunissent
Le soleil brille dans nos villes

Notre fenêtre s'écarquille
Jusqu'à refléter l'avenir

Tuiles d'avoir vu rose dans l'exaltation
De l'azur un enfant se disperse et se cherche

Les nuages ne pèsent rien
L'orage nerveux les décoiffe

L'air et l'eau coulent dans nos mains
Comme verdure en notre cœur

Le sang d'un homme est un fuseau
Si serré qu'il n'en finit pas

Je ne me suis jamais fait à l'image exacte
Qu'un miroir me renvoie sans prévoir mes grimaces

Statue there remains but one for us to see
It is the proud bearing of man on earth

A single roof unites all skies
Each house is but a work of fancy

The horizon reaches my eyes
By what miracle could I be afraid

Space is a trickle of milk
That feeds and nourishes me

Panorama at the bottom of a deep well
I gaze at a sky replete with stars and reflections

Star adds to stars
We know how to blend the seasons

We know how to untie the knots
Of what are only chance events

The old snows revive
The sun shines into our towns

Our windows fling open wide
Until they display the future

Bad luck to have seen the rosy side
In the joy of the sky a child runs off and feels its way

The clouds have no weight
The rumbling storm blows them away

Air and water flow through our hands
Like greenness into our hearts

The blood of a man is a spindle
So packed that it never stops turning

I never could see myself in the absolute image
That a mirror returns not expecting the faces I pull

Une flèche s'épanouit
De l'arc du lit de la fatigue

Contre la mort la vieille histoire
Dont la gloire s'est effacée

La griffe agrafe l'or fragile
Du clair mirage de sa proie

La liane enlace la foule
L'épi fertilise la foudre

Le miel crispe un faisceau d'aiguilles
Qui cousent la douceur de vivre

La perle morte se divise
En mille perles feux fertiles

La perle parle par l'éclat de sa candeur
Quand donc n'aurai-je plus qu'à me fondre en la mienne

Feux des minutes feux des îles
Au long d'un voyage immobile

D'un grand voyage où nul n'est seul
Où nul n'a peur de son prochain

Routes je suis au pas des hommes les meilleurs
Routes je vais plus loin que ce que j'espérais

Il m'a toujours fallu un seul être pour vivre
Pour exalter les autres

Pierre je ne suis pas de bois
Ma chair est bouillante et vivace

Nos mains sont menées à la danse
Par l'aile et le chant des oiseaux

La table règle l'écriture
Le fin propos la note juste

An arrow flares
From the bow of the bed of weariness

Against death the old story
Whose glory has dimmed

The claw holds down the brittle gold
Of the clear mirage of its prey

The creeper fastens around the crowd
The ear of corn enriches the lightning

The honey shrivels a cluster of needles
That sew together the sweetness of living

The dead pearl breaks
Into a thousand pearls like fertile fires

The pearl speaks through the shine of its artlessness
When shall I need but to vanish into mine

Fires of the minutes fires of the islands
All through a journey that never began

A great journey where no one is alone
Where no one fears his neighbour

Roads   I am in step with the best of men
Roads   I travel farther than I had hoped

I have always needed one being to live
To live and dignify others

Stone I am not made of wood
My flesh seethes and is everlasting

Our hands are led to the dance
By the wing and the song of birds

The table defines the writing
The shrewd remark the right note

La table règle la moisson
Comme nos lèvres le plaisir

La marée monte comme l'arbre
Comme nos yeux qui se répandent

La voile fait un pas immense
Puis se gonfle pour tous les vents

Une voile s'en va revient gagne le large
Diminué à ma vue et grandit à l'escale

L'homme navigue et vole il dénoue la distance
Il élude son poids il échappe à la terre

Je peux vivre entre quatre murs
Sans rien oublier du dehors

Chambre de l'ancien temps noyau d'un fruit géant
J'ouvre la porte qui en sort les fous les sages

Tous plus beaux les uns que les autres
Chacun devançant le matin

Tremplin mur renversé de la prison des pauvres
Libres les pauvres se confondent

Ils ont tous la même richesse
Pour s'entr'aimer plus près d'eux-mêmes

Pour s'entr'aider le seul poème
Vraiment rythmé vraiment rimé

Chacun a découvert son bien
Et le bien de tous est sans ombre

Il nous suffit d'être chacun pour être tous
D'être soi-même pour nous sentir entre nous

D'être sages pour être fous
Et d'être fous pour être sages

The table defines the harvest
Like our lips the pleasure

The tide rises like the tree
Like our eyes that cast around

The sail heaves
Then swells to catch every wind

A sail vanishes returns takes to the open sea
Grows smaller in my sight and greater lying at anchor

Man steers and flies solves the riddle of space
Breaks free from his weight escapes from earth

I can live between four walls
Without forgetting the world outside

Room of former times stone of a giant fruit
I open the door and there come the mad and the wise

All of them noble some more than others
Each of them outruns the morning

A place to jump is the wall of a prison torn down
As free men the poor become confused

They all have the same means
To love one another those close by

To help one another the only poem
Truly in rhythm truly in rhyme

Each has discovered his riches
And the common good is shadowless

It is enough to be one to be everyone
To be oneself to feel the warmth of men

To be wise to be mad
To be mad to be wise

Viens à côté de moi toi qui passais au large
Je m'approche de toi moi qui sors de la foule

D'une caresse au seuil de notre nudité
L'univers s'impose subtil

D'une caresse au seuil de nos premiers baisers
Nous passons aux plus fines branches

Un amour qui n'a pas de but
Sinon la vie sans différences

L'extase en est légère à nos sens rassemblés
Comme l'aube à nos rêves

À nos sens rassemblés

Il nous faut voir toucher sentir goûter entendre
Pour allumer un feu sous le ciel blanc et bleu
Toujours le premier feu l'étoile sur la terre
Et la première fleur dans notre corps naissant

Sens de tous les instants

Il nous faut voir ne pas voir noir être confiant
Et de la vue sauvage faire une lumière
Sans fumée et sans cruauté
Tu la respires et ton souffle me libère

Mes yeux ont su te sourire

J'ai rempli la coupe d'eau
J'ai rempli la plaine d'hommes
Je me suis comblé d'aurore
Et de sang j'ai vu en moi

Voir se limite à la paume
Des orbites golfe idéal

Rose haute de la marée
Tous mes désirs abreuvés
Rose avouée en pleurant

Come to my side you who were passing by
I am coming to you I who emerge from the crowd

With an embrace on the threshold of our nakedness
Delicately the world intrudes

With an embrace on the threshold of our first kisses
We continue our way to the tenderest flowers

A love that has no purpose
Unless it is life without differences

Rapture lies lightly on our senses come together
Like the dawn on our dreams

On our senses come together

We must see touch smell taste hear
To light a fire under the sky of blue and cloud
The first fire the star over the earth
And the first flower in our bodies coming to life

Senses for every fleeting moment

We must see clearly never darkly be confiding
From what we find in nature light a fire
That does not smoke that does not sear
You breathe it in and your breath will set me free

My eyes have learned to smile upon you

I have filled the cup with water
I have filled the plain with men
I have drunk my fill of dawn
And blood have seen within myself

Seen confined in the palm of my hand
A perfect sweep of water

Rose of a compass high above the tide
All my wishes satisfied
A rose confessed in tears

Apprends à tout me dire je peux tout entendre
Ta pensée est sans honte pense à haute voix

Silence la merveille simple
Et de fil en aiguille
Tout s'est épanoui
Le vent obscurément nettoie
La mer et le soleil

Ton souffle gonfle mes réponses
Entends le vent je sais ce que tu dis
Et je me lie aux bruits qui te font vivre
Sur une route où l'écho bat dans tous les cœurs
Malgré la porte et les volets fermés
Ma timide écoutons le tonnerre des bruits
Et les muets cherchant à dissiper leur nuit
Écoutons ce qui dort en nous d'inexprimé

Franchissons nos limites

J'étais loin j'avais faim j'avais soif d'un contact

Te toucher ressemblait aux terres fécondées
Aux terres épuisées
Par l'effort des charrues des pluies et des étés
Te toucher composait un visage de feuilles
Un corps d'herbes un corps couché dans un buisson
Ta main m'a protégé des orties et des ronces
Mes caresses fondaient mes reves en un seul
Clairvoyant et aveugle un rêve de durée

Car je te touchais mieux la nuit

J'étais sauvé

D'avoir goûté le ciel la terre et la marée
Senti le sang la peau la gelée et le foin
D'avoir tout entendu touché je me montrais
Je respirais me colorais marchais parlais
Et me reproduisais

Learn to tell me everything I can hear everything
Your thoughts are shameless think your thoughts aloud

Silence the simple miracle
And slowly but surely
Everything has blossomed
Unseen the wind sweeps
The sea and the sun

Your breath makes grander my replies
Listen to the wind I know what you are saying
I stop to listen to the sounds that bring you alive
Along a road where the echo beats in every heart
Despite the shutters and the door shut fast
My shy one let us listen to the rolling sounds
And the silences that try to drive away the night
Listen to what within us sleeps unsaid

Let us break through bounds

I was far away I hungered I thirsted for a presence

To touch you was to touch the lands made lush
The lands made sparse
By the work of plough of rain of summers
To touch you was to paint an image of leaves
A body of grasses a body at rest in a brake
Your hand protected me from nettles and thorns
My kisses dissolved my dreams into a single dream
Sighted and sightless a dream to last

Because to touch you was more real in the night

I was saved

Because I had relished sky and earth and tide
Smelled blood and skin and frost and hay
Heard and touched everything I could be seen
I breathed decked myself in colours walked and talked
And was born again

D'avoir vu clair en plein midi j'acceptais l'ombre
Je savais diviser et grouper les étoiles
Et les actes des hommes
Je savais être moins et bien plus que moi-même
Mes cinq sens faisaient place à l'imagination

> *L'imagination laisse à penser*
> *Que nous possédons un sixième sens.*

Les cinq sens confondus c'est l'imagination
Qui voit qui sent qui touche qui entend qui goûte
Qui prolonge l'instinct qui précise les routes
Du désir ambitieux
Je sais la vérité dès que je l'imagine
Le mal étant à vaincre

J'imagine je vois le dessous le dessus
D'un pont qui joint les hommes
D'un pont qui joint les mondes
Je vois la rose sourdre d'une pierre morne
La panthère atterrir au delà du désordre
Des rochers et des ronces

Je vois l'enfant pétrir le pain de l'avenir
La femme dans la paix de son cœur s'offrir nue
Ou bien vêtue de tout
J'imagine l'écho du premier cri d'espoir
Le premier feu passant d'une main à une autre
Le dernier mot des fous

Les fruits ont la saveur de l'aube associée
Aux lèvres des plus fraîches sources
J'imagine et j'en perds le souffle
Que rayonne un arc de concorde
Des plus hauts besoins des esclaves
À la force qui les délivre

Je vois ce monde tel qu'il fut dans ses vitrines
Figé prudent et puis il roule dans la rue
Il éclabousse les pavés
Il glisse à la passion des terres cultivées
Comme un sein débridé par des mains appliquées
Je suis fait pour boire son lait j'en ai le droit

Because I was not blind I accepted the dark
I knew how to separate and group the stars
And the deeds of men
I could be less and bigger than I was
My five senses yielded to imagination

Imagination leads us to believe
we possess a sixth sense

The five senses all together are imagination
That sees that smells that touches hears and tastes
That magnifies instinct that maps the roads
Of ambitious desire
I know the truth as soon as I conceive it
The false is there to be overcome

I imagine and see the shape
Of a bridge that unites men
Of a bridge that unites worlds
I see the rose rise from a colourless stone
The panther drop to ground beyond the confusion
Of rock and thorn

I see the child kneading the bread of the future
The woman in the peace of her heart who offers herself
Naked or fully clothed
I imagine the echo of the first cry of hope
The first fire passing from hand to hand
The last word of the mad

Fruits have the relish of dawn that tastes
Like lips from the coolest wells
I imagine then I let go the ecstasy
That sends into space an arch of harmony
From the greater needs of slaves
To the force that sets them free

I see this world as it was displayed
Still and cautious then hurrying through the streets
It spatters the paving-stones
It races to the passion of ploughed fields
Like a breast assaulted by questing hands
I am made to drink its milk it is my right

Je vois ce monde qui n'est pas mais qui sera
Ce monde qui a tout pour lui
Il a la mère il a la graine
Il sait construire des palais
Il sait ce qui est inutile
Ses chaînes tiennent à un fil

Demain je ne périrai pas
Demain je suis mon enchanteur
Demain le feu baise mes pas
Et la sécheresse renonce
La rosée de mon cœur éclaire
Ce qu'aucun homme n'a pu voir

Mais tout n'a pas été si facile ni gai

Et je veux dire ce qui est à cet instant
Où tout à tout jamais semble buter sur l'ombre

L'enfant pâlit terriblement devant son père
L'enfant ne lutte pas n'a pas le torse nu
Ni les poings pétrifiés ni le cœur endurci
Ni les yeux éduqués ni la parole faite

Sa chaleur maigre et glabre
N'alimente pas le foyer
Et puisqu'il est sans créatures
Il se rêve sans créateur

Je vois un lac très fin qui s'éveille trop tôt
J'oublie vite la masse de la sympathie
J'ai trente-six façons de ne rien annoncer
Puisqu'hier j'étais jeune aujourd'hui je suis jeune

Je ne veux pas grandir je ne veux rien apprendre
Ma forge est plus fragile que ses étincelles
Je m'exprime par bonds sans savoir où je vais
Quand je me sens perdu enfin je me repose

Comme un désert inexploré
L'enfant pâlit terriblement

I see this world not as it is but will be
This world that is blessed with everything
It has mothers it has seed
It can build palaces
It knows what is worthless
Its chains hang by a thread

Tomorrow I shall not perish
Tomorrow I shall be my enchanter
Tomorrow the fire will bless the ground I tread
And the drought will surrender
The dew of my heart will throw its light
On what no man could see

But not everything was so easy or free of care

And I mean what is happening here and now
Where everything seems to beat against the dark

The child pales in terror in front of his father
The child does not struggle has no will to fight
No clenched fists no hardened heart
No eyes of experience no ready word

His weak and boyish warmth
Does not feed the fire
And since he has no fellow creatures
He dreams of himself without a creator

I see a very clear lake that stirs too soon
Quickly I forget the store of responsiveness
I have a hundred ways of declaring nothing
Since yesterday I was young today I am still young

I do not want to grow I do not want to learn
My forge is less substantial than its sparks
I jump about at random not knowing where I go
When I feel lost is when I rest

Like a desert unexplored
The child pales in terror

Ai-je jamais été enfant
Moi qui peux parler de l'enfance
Comme je parle de la mort

J'invente mon enfance et j'invente la mort
Passant je m'asphyxie d'être naissant mourant
Et je cherche à me joindre ailleurs à une autre heure

Où ai-je commencé quelle fin franchirai-je
Je refuse l'instant qui me prouve semblable
À toutes mes images faites ou défaites

Je n'ai pas été jeune et je ne mourrai pas

La joie de vivre est un fruit mûr
Que le soleil glace de sucre

Et le printemps est dans l'hiver
Et sur ma mémoire ensablée
Mirage passe un appel d'air
Plénitude plane un oiseau

Je souffre de ne pas savoir
Quand je suis né quand je mourrai
Je souffre d'être sans limites
Je confonds hier et demain
Mes soirs mes matins sont changeants
Je me perds et je m'éternise
Au carrefour de leurs reflets

Je ne suis pas comme une plante
Pendu au temps qu'il fait

Je ne suis pas comme un insecte
Absorbé par le sol

Quand je vole je vais plus droit
Que la mouette ou l'hirondelle

D'un fer pesant d'un fer ardent
Je repasse les plis du vent

Was I ever a child
I who can speak of childhood
As I speak of death

I invent my childhood and I invent death
Then I stifle for being born and dying
And I try to belong elsewhere in another time

Where did I begin what end shall I reach
I spurn the moment that proves me like
The images I made of me and then destroyed

I was never young and I shall not die

The joy of living is a ripe fruit
That the sun coats with sweetness

And spring is there within winter
And over my blinded memory
Illusion sends a rush of air
Abundance soars like a bird

I agonise not knowing
When I was born when I shall die
I agonise for want of bounds
Yesterday and tomorrow I confuse
My nights my mornings are fickle
I lose my way spend endless hours
Where their reflections cross each other

I am not like a plant
At the mercy of the weather as it comes

I am not like an insect
Sucked into the soil

When I fly I travel straighter
Than the seagull or the swallow

With a heavy iron with a burning iron
I flatten the folds of the wind

Je n'ai vraiment plus besoin d'ailes
Pour calciner ma pesanteur

Et je peux creuser dans la terre
Des puits plus musclés que ma force

Et je peux tirer de mon cœur
Le temps d'être toujours meilleur

Je vis à l'échelle de tous
Ce qui me manque un autre l'a

Chacun sait lire de confiance
La loi qui ne courbe personne

Je prends n'importe quel visage
Comme une goutte d'apparence

Pour animer tous les visages
Et pour commencer par un seul

Je construis l'amour au sommet
D'un univers porteur d'espoir

Nous sommes l'un et l'autre au jour
Pour n'en jamais finir d'aimer

Pour ne plus jamais renoncer
À la fraternité

Pourtant ce monde est petit
Petit comme une journée

Petit comme un nom banal
Comme une feuille d'automne

L'enfant dans l'épicerie
Répète ses commissions

Et puis il compte ses sous
L'amant pense à son travail

Really I have no need of wings
To burn off my heaviness

And I can dig out of earth
Wells sturdier than my strength

And I can drag from my heart
The time to do better still

I live in the way that others live
What I lack another has

Each can read with trust
The law that humbles no one

I accept whatever face there is
As a semblance of truth

To light up every face
And to begin with just one

I build love at the mountain top
Of a world that is bearer of hope

We are in daylight each one of us
For never ceasing to love

For never more to abandon
Brotherhood

Yet this world is small
Small as a passing day

Small as a simple name
As an autumn leaf

The child in the grocery store
Reads out his shopping list

And then he counts his money
The lover thinks about his work

Le savant pense à son train
L'ouvrier à l'hôpital

La rue passe son chiffon
Sur les pas des hommes las

Le poète veut manger
La putain veut réussir

Une hache va tomber
Sur le cou des condamnés

Le héros est privé d'armes
La mère est lasse à mourir

Le sommeil les réunit
L'aube les éveille à peine

La fatigue les dissout
La misère les sépare

Je vois le dos d'un manteau gris
Dans une rue très basse sous la pluie

Je vois des pygmées sans conscience
Saluer leurs drapeaux en priant

Je vois des soldats dans la boue
Saluer les balles de la tête

Je vois les maisons démolies
Comme à plaisir pour une fête

Je vois un ventre ouvert en grand
Aux mouches au soleil pourri

Je vois les mains estropiées
Des vieillards menés à l'asile

Je vois des beautés inutiles
S'éteindre dans la nuit du doute

The scholar thinks about his train
The worker about the hospital

The street wipes its rag
Over the tread of weary men

The poet wants to eat
The whore means to succeed

An axe is going to fall
On the necks of condemned men

The hero is deprived of weapons
The mother is weary to death

Sleep brings them together
Dawn barely arouses them

Fatigue dispels them
Distress keeps them apart

I see the back of a grey cloak
In a very low street in the rain

I see mindless little men
Salute their flags by praying

I see soldiers in the mud
Salute bullets with a nod of the head

I see houses destroyed
Wantonly for celebration

I see a stomach opened wide
To flies in the scorching sun

I see the crippled hands
Of old men led to sanctuary

I see useless beauties
Extinguished in the night of doubt

Et les fleurs sont artificielles
Et la terre devient stérile

Et je devrais bientôt me taire

Pourtant si je suis sur la terre
C'est que d'autres y sont aussi
Qui comme moi ont bégayé
Quand nous n'étions tout à fait muets

Il faut leur rendre la parole
Ils ont avalé le poison
Maudit leur mère et leur misère
Sans rien connaître d'exaltant

Il ne faut promettre et donner
La vie que pour la perpétuer
Comme on perpétue une rose
En l'encerclant de mains heureuses.

And the flowers are not real
And earth becomes barren

Soon I must say nothing

Yet if I walk the earth
The reason is that others too are there
Who like me spoke haltingly
When we were not entirely silent

To them we must return their speech
They have swallowed the poison
Cursed their mothers and misfortunes
Not knowing reasons to make glad

Life we must only promise and give
So that it will endure
As we cherish the life of a rose
Cupping it with happy hands.

BLASON DÉDORÉ DE MES RÊVES
TARNISHED EMBLEMS OF MY DREAMS

Dans ce rêve et pourtant j'étais presque éveillé
Je me croyais au seuil de la grande avalanche
Tête d'air renversée sous le poids de la terre
Ma trace était déjà dissipée j'étouffais
Dernier souffle premier gouffre définitif

Je respire souvent très mal je me confine
Moralement aussi surtout quand je suis seul

Dans ce rêve le temps de vivre était réduit
À sa plus simple expression naître et mourir
Mes vertèbres mes nerfs ma chair
Tremblaient bégayaient d'ignorance
Et je perdais mon apparence

J'en vins pour me sauver à rêver d'animaux
De chiens errants et fous de nocturnes immenses
D'insectes de bois sec et de grappes gluantes
Et de masses mouvantes
Plus confuses que des rochers
Plus compliquées que la forêt d'outre-chaleur
Où le soleil se glisse comme une névrite
Des animaux cachots tunnels et labyrinthes
Sur terre et sous terre oubliés
Des animaux au sein de l'eau qui les nourrit
À fleur de l'air qui les contient
Et des animaux décantés
Faits de tout et de rien
Comme les astres supposés
Sans parois immédiates sans rapports certains
Vertige dans la brume je restais en friche

Je figurais comme un mendiant
La nature et les éléments
Et ma chair pauvre mon sang riche
Et mes plumes vives fanées
Mes écailles ma peau vidée
Ma voix muette mon cœur sourd
Mon pelage mes griffes sûres
Ma course et mon cheminement
Ma ponte et mon éventrement

In this dream and yet I was almost awake
I thought I was on the shelf of a great avalanche
My empty head spilled under the weight of the earth
My tracks had already blown away I choked
A last gasp and then the first chasm opening

Often I breathe very badly withdraw into myself
Morally too and mostly when alone

In this dream existence was reduced
To its simplest terms of birth and death
My bones my nerves my flesh
Trembled and failed for want of understanding
And I lost all sense of self

To save myself I took to dreaming of animals
Of wild dogs maddened in immense night scenes
Of insects in dry wood and slimy clusters
And drifting blocks
More undefined than rocks
More tortuous than the steaming forest
Where the sun steals through a turbulence
Of animals prisons tunnels and winding paths
Forgotten above and below the ground
Animals deep in the water they drink
Or gliding through air that holds them up
And animals settling down to rest
Made of everything and nothing
Like heavenly bodies believed to be
Without shape or size no part of a system
My head was swimming so I lay fallow

Like a beggar I imagined
Nature and the elements
My poor flesh my thick blood
And my shiny feathers drooping
My scales my shrivelled skin
My silent voice my slow heart
My plumage my sharp claws
My racing around my slow progress
My giving birth and my disembowelment

Ma mue et ma mort sans rupture
Mon corps absurde prisonnier
Des poussées de la vie en vrac
Ma fonction d'être reproduit
Interminablement
M'inclinaient toujours un peu plus
Vers le fond le plus inconscient

J'en vins pour me sauver à me croire animal
Voguent volent se terrent mes frissons d'enfant
Mes yeux jamais ouverts et mon vagissement
Je ne refuse pas l'hiver je vis encore
Dans l'embrasure de l'automne mais je passe
Aux premiers froids comme une feuille
Ou bien je meurs comme je nais sans majesté
Dans un gargouillement je suis la bulle éclose
Et crevée au soleil je tisse sans savoir
La toile la fourrure ou le bond sans fêlure
Qui me permettent de durer pour un instant
Nul n'a jamais ri ni pleuré
Je ne m'embourbe ni n'étouffe
Je ne me brûle ni me noie
Je suis le nombre indéfini
Au cœur d'une page de chiffres

Je suis fils de mes origines
J'en ai les rides les ravines
Le sang léger la sève épaisse
Les sommets flous les caves sombres
La rosée et la rouille
Je m'équilibre et je chavire
Comme les couches de terrain
Et je m'étale et je me traîne
Je brûle et je gèle à jamais
Et je suis insensible
Car mes sens engloutissent
La chute et l'ascension
La fleur et sa racine
Le ver et son cocon
Le diamant et la mine
L'œil et son horizon

My moulting and my death without a stop
My absurd body a prisoner
Of the random thrusts of life
My purpose to be reproduced
Interminably
Were pushing me closer and closer
To a distant place of unconsciousness

To save myself I took to believing I was animal
My childish shivers come and drift and vanish
My eyes never open and my wailing
I do not recoil from winter I am still alive
In the open space of autumn but I arrive
At the first chills like a leaf
Or I die as I am born lacking dignity
In a squelch I am a bubble burst
And burnt in the sun I weave unaware
The cloth the fur the perfect leap
That help me to endure a moment more
No one has ever laughed or cried
I do not flounder nor do I choke
I do not burn nor do I drown
I am the casual number
In a mass of many numbers

I am the son of the way I began
I bear its lines and furrows
The thin blood the thick sap
The misty heights the dark caves
The dew and the blight
I sway and I collapse
Like layers of the land
And I stretch and I crawl
I burn and freeze all the time
I am unfeeling
For my senses all misuse
The descent and the ascent
The flower and its root
The worm and its cocoon
The diamond and its mine
The eye and its horizon

Je ne suis ni lourd ni léger
Ni solitaire ni peuplé
Nul ne peut séparer
Ma chevelure de mes bras
Ni ma gorge de son silence
Ni ma lumière de ma nuit
Je suis la foule partout
Des profondeurs et des hauteurs
La grimace en creux en relief
La crispation de la distance
La clarté close ou provocante
Le masque posé sur la nacre
La glèbe creusée par la taupe
La vague enflée par le requin
La brise chantante d'oiseaux
Pour rien pour que tout continue
Dans un foyer brillant éteint
Et ranimé par un fétu

Les animaux sont la charnière
Des ailerons du mouvement
Ils ne connaissent ni naufrages
Ni décombres ils perpétuent
La longue alliance de la boue
Avec l'azur avec la pierre
Avec le flot avec la flamme
Dure et douce comme une bouche
Je ne peux pas me reposer
Je m'agrège au jeu sans issue
Au bruit sans couleur de musique
Il n'est pas question de régner
Ni de parler pour troubler l'ordre insane

Ni d'élever le talus te mon crâne
Plus haut que le buisson du jour
Ni de permettre à ma poitrine
Par son étrave de troubler
La lie de l'immobilité

Animal je n'ai rien qui me conduise ailleurs

110

I am neither heavy nor light
Neither alone nor in the crowd
No one can tear
The hair from my arms
Nor my throat from its silence
Nor my light from my darkness
Everywhere I am the throng
Of the depths and heights
The gesture hollow or with meaning
The shrivelling of distance
The brightness darkening or enticing
The mask that rests upon the pearl
The soil that is dug by the mole
The wave that is swelled by the shark
The breeze that is singing with birds
For nothing so that everything endures
In a blazing fire extinguished
And revived by a flicker

Animals it is they
Who make the wings of movement work
They know neither wastage
Nor disaster they perpetuate
The long collusion of the mire
With the blue sky with the stone
With the flood with the flame
Hard and soft like a mouth
I cannot rest
I join the game that offers no escape
And the sound without colour of music
There is no question of mastery
Nor of speech to disturb the madness

Nor of lifting the thoughts in my head
Higher than the outline of the day
Nor of allowing my breast
By its heaving to disturb
The dregs of stillness

Animal I have nothing that might lead me on elsewhere

Je ne dispose pas du temps il est entier
Ma poussière ignore les routes
La foudre anime mon squelette
Et la foudre m'immobilise
Je suis pour un printemps le battement de l'aile
Je glisse et passe sur l'air lisse
Je suis rompu par le fer rouge
De l'aurore et du crépuscule
La terre absorbe mon reflet
Je ne suis l'objet d'aucun doute
Je ne contemple rien je guette
La prolifération de l'ombre
Où je puis être et m'abolir
L'envie m'en vient sans réfléchir
Le mur que je frappe m'abat
Et je tombe et je me relève
Dans le même abîme essentiel
Dans la même absence d'images

Dessus dessous la vérité élémentaire
La vérité sans son contraire
Il n'est pas une erreur au monde
Le jour banal et la nuit ordinaire
Et des attaches pour toujours
Avec un point fixe la vie
Ni bonne ni mauvaise
Une vie absorbant la mort
Sans apparence de prestige

Nulle auréole pour le lion
Nul ongle d'or pour l'aigle
Et les hyènes n'ont pas de honte
Les poissons s'ignorent nageant
Aucun oiseau ne vole
Le lièvre court pour mettre un point
Au regard fixe de la chouette
L'araignée ne fait qu'une toile
Utile ou inutile un grenier une ruine

Time is not mine it is complete
My dust knows nothing of roads
The lightning shakes my skeleton
And the lightning holds me fast
For one spring I am the beating of a wing
I glide and drift through the soft air
I am deadened by the angry red
Of the dawn and dusk
The earth absorbs my reflection
I am not cursed by any doubt
I contemplate nothing I lie in wait
For the swarming of the shades
Where I can stop and disappear
It comes to desire without a thought
The wall I strike at throws me to the ground
And I fall and rise again
In the same absolute chasm
In the same place empty of image

All around the elementary truth
The truth without its opposite
There is no mistake in nature
The typical day and the usual night
And never-ending fetters
Settle this life with a definition
Neither good nor bad
A life that has death within itself
Without a semblance of mystiquê

No glory for the lion
No claw of gold for the eagle
And the hyenas have no shame
The fish are unaware they swim
No bird flies
The hare races to come to a stop
Under the stare of the owl
The spider spins only one web
To use or not a store or a disaster

Je me sens m'en aller très bas
Très haut très près très loin très flou
Et net immense et plus petit
Que le ciel amassé pour moi
J'imite le plus machinal
Des gestes d'un lieudit la terre
Lune et soleil sont sans mystère
Non plus que l'épaule aux aisselles
Non plus que le vent à mes ailes

Blason dédoré de mes rêves
Ai-je fait mon deuil de moi-même

En me couchant comme la cendre sous la flamme
Ai-je abdiqué ne puis-je plus rien désigner
En me montrant du doigt moi si fier d'être au monde

Non je dors et malgré le pouvoir de la nuit
J'apprends comme un enfant que je vais m'éveiller
Mes draps sont le linceul de mes rêves je vis

Et du gouffre je passe à la lumière blonde
Et je respire comme un amoureux se pâme
Comme un fleuve se tisse sous une hirondelle

Je sais que je ne suis pas seul ma fièvre augmente
Je m'élance et je monte et j'affirme mon but
Je suis enfin sorti de mon sommeil je vis.

I feel myself drifting very low down very high up
Very near and very far and everything very blurred
And clearly huge yet smaller
Than the sky that has gathered for me
I imitate the most unthinking
Movements of a place called earth
Moon and sun have no mystery
No more than the purpose of my limbs
No more than the wind on my wings

Tarnished emblems of my dreams
Have I done my mourning for myself

When I lay down like ashes under the flame
Did I yield can I no more choose anything
By pointing at myself I so proud to exist

No I sleep and for all the power of the night
I learn like a child that I shall wake
My sheets are the shroud of my dreams I am alive

And from the abyss I come to the shining light
And I breathe like a lover who swoons
Like a river ruffling under a swallow's flight

I know I am not alone my fever rises
I leap and I soar and assert myself
I have at last emerged from sleep I am alive

NOTE:

Paul Éluard écrivit les *Épitaphes* au cours de l'été 1952,
avant d'avoir ressenti les premières atteintes du mal
qui devait l'emporter.

Paul Éluard wrote this poem during the summer of 1952
before suffering the first effects of a fatal illness.

ÉPITAPHES

EPITAPHS

L'epigramme funéraire est un antique
moyen de donner à penser aux vivants.
Par-dessus le mur du passé, elle peut
transmettre la confiance et l'espoir.

I

(pour Marc)

L'enfant j'ai été l'enfant
Joue sans jamais réfléchir
Aux sombres détours du temps

Éternel il joue pour rire
Il conserve son printemps
Son ruisseau est un torrent

Moi mon plaisir fut délire
Mais je suis mort à neuf ans.

II

La souffrance est comme un ciseau
Qui tranche dans la chair vivante
Et j'en ai subi l'épouvante
Comme de la flèche à l'oiseau
Du feu du désert à la plante
Comme la glace sur les eaux

Mon cœur a subi les injures
Du malheur et de l'injustice
Je vivais en un temps impur
Où certains faisaient leurs délices
D'oublier leurs frères leurs fils
Le hasard m'a clos dans ses murs

Mais dans ma nuit je n'ai rêvé que de l'azur.

*

Je pouvais tout et je ne pouvais rien
Je pouvais tout aimer mais pas assez.

*

*In times past the speaking of epigrams at
burials was a custom used to inspire in
mourners a sense of confidence and hope
in the future.*

I

(for Marc)

The child I was the child
Plays without ever thinking about
The unlit turnings of time

Never ending he plays for fun
He keeps safe his spring
His stream is a torrent

My pleasures were sheer delight
But I died when I was nine.

II

Pain is like a knife
That cuts into living flesh
And I suffered the agony of pain
Like the bird the shock of the arrow
Like the plant the heat of the desert
Like ice on the water

My heart suffered the wrongs
Of injustice and unhappiness
I lived in an unclean time
When some would find their pleasure
By forgetting their sons and brothers
Chance sealed me in its walls

But in my nights I dreamed only of the blue sky.

*

I could do anything I could do nothing
I could love anything but not enough.

*

Le ciel la mer la terre
M'ont englouti

L'homme m'a fait renaître.

*

Ci-gît celui qui vécut sans douter
Que l'aube est bonne à tous les âges
Quand il mourut il pensa naître
Car le soleil recommençait.

*

J'ai vécu fatigué pour moi et pour les autres
Mais j'ai toujours voulu soulager mes épaules
Et les épaules de mes frères les plus pauvres
De ce commun fardeau qui nous mène à la tombe
Au nom de mon espoir je m'inscris contre l'ombre.

*

Arrête-toi et souviens-toi de la forêt
De la prairie plus claire sous le soleil vif
Souviens-toi des regards sans brumes sans remords

Le mien s'est effacé le tien l'a remplacé
D'avoir été d'être vivants nous continuons
Nous couronnons le désir d'être et de durer.

III

Ceux qui m'ont mis à mort ceux qui ne redoutaient
Que de manquer mon cœur tu les as oubliés

Je suis dans ton présent comme y est la lumière
Comme un homme vivant qui n'a chaud que sur terre

Seuls mon espoir et mon courage sont restés
Tu prononces mon nom et tu respires mieux

J'avais confiance en toi nous sommes généreux
Nous avançons le bonheur brûle le passé

Et notre force rajeunit dans tous les yeux.

Sky sea earth
Swamped over me

Man brought me to life again.

*

Here lies one who lived never doubting
That dawn is good at every age
When he died he thought of birth
For the sun was rising again.

*

I lived tired for myself and others
But I always wished to free my shoulders
And the shoulders of my poorest brothers
Of that burden we all bear that leads us to the grave
For my hope's sake I set my face against the dark.

*

Stop and remember the forest
The meadow brightest in the shining sun
Remember the faces without remorse or mist of tears

Mine faded away yours took its place
For this survival we alive remain
We crown the wish to last and to abide.

III

You have forgotten them those who put me to death
Those who feared only to lack my heart

I am in your every day as the light is there
Like a living man who is only warm on earth

Only my hope and my courage have remained
You utter my name and you breathe more freely

I had believed in you we are bountiful
We go our way and happiness burns the past

And our strength grows younger for all to see.

ABOLIR LES MYSTÈRES
DOING AWAY WITH MYSTERIES

Ce ne sont pas mains de géants

Ce ne sont pas mains de géants
Ce ne sont pas mains de génies
Qui ont forgé nos chaînes ni le crime

Ce sont des mains habituées à elles-mêmes
Vides d'amour vides du monde
Le commun des mortels ne les a pas serrées

Elles sont devenues aveugles étrangères
À tout ce qui n'est pas bêtement une proie
Leur plaisir s'assimile au feu nu du désert

Leurs dix doigts multiplient des zéros dans des comptes
Qui ne mènent à rien qu'au fin fond des faillites
Et leur habileté les comble de néant

Ces mains sont à la poupe au lieu d'être à la proue
Au crépuscule au lieu d'être à l'aube éclatante
Et divisant l'élan annulent tout espoir

Ce ne sont que des mains condamnées de tout temps
Par la foule joyeuse qui descend du jour
Où chacun pourrait être juste à tout jamais

Et rire de savoir qu'il n'est pas seul sur terre
À vouloir se conduire en vertu de ses frères
Pour un bonheur unique où rire est une loi

Il faut entre nos mains qui sont les plus nombreuses
Broyer la mort idiote abolir les mystères
Construire la raison de naître et vivre heureux.

It is not the hands of giants

It is not the hands of giants
It is not the hands of genius
That forged our chains nor is it crime

It is hands that share with no one
Loveless bereft of this world
The common run of mortals did not shake them

They have become strangers blind
To everything not foolishly a prey
Their pleasure is like the naked desert fire

Their ten fingers grow by noughts in ledgers
Leading to nowhere but the deeps of failure
And their tricks pile nothingness upon them

These hands are on the stern and not the prow
At dusk and not the flaring break of day
Spirit they break apart to blot out every hope

They are simply hands damned all the time
By the happy crowd that marches to the day
When every man could be just for evermore

And laugh at knowing he is not alone on earth
Wanting to live a life designed for brothers
For happiness entire where laughter is a law

We must between our hands which are in greater numbers
Crush to nothing senseless death do away with mysteries
Build reasons for being born and living happily.

Les constructeurs

(à Fernand Léger)

Pleurez vieux paresseux des temps incohérents
Vos prétentions nous feront rire
Nous avons fait notre ciment
De la poussière du désert
Nos roses sont écloses comme un vin soûlant
Nos yeux sont des fenêtres propres
Dans le visage blond des maisons du soleil

Et nous chantons en force comme des géants

Nos mains sont les étoiles de notre drapeau
Nous avons conquis notre toit le toit de tous
Et notre cœur monte et descend dans l'escalier
Flamme de mort et fraîcheur de naissance
Nous avons construit des maisons
Pour y dépenser la lumière
Pour que la nuit ne coupe plus la vie en deux

Chez nous l'amour grandit quand nos enfants s'élèvent

Gagner manger comme on gagne la paix
Gagner aimer comme le printemps gagne
Quand nous parlons nous entendons
La vérité des charpentiers
Des maçons des couvreurs des sages
Ils ont porté le monde au-dessus de la terre
Au-dessus des prisons des tombeaux des cavernes

Contre toute fatigue ils jurent de durer.

The builders

(to Fernand Léger)

Weep old lazy bones for the lazy times
Your swank will make us laugh
We have made our cement
With the desert sand
Our roses are blooming like a heady wine
Our eyes are clean windows
In the bright face of the mansions of the sun

And we sing like giants with all our might

Our hands are the stars in our flag
We have scaled our roofs a roof for everyone
And our hearts go up and down the stairs
Flame of death and freshness of birth
We have built houses
To let the light flood in
So darkness shall never again cut life in two

With us love grows when our children rise

To earn to eat as we earn peace
To earn to love as springtime overtakes
When we talk we hear
The truth from carpenters
From masons roofers from good men
They have lifted the world above the ground
High above prisons tombs and cellars

Despite all weariness they swear to endure.

LE CHÂTEAU DES PAUVRES
THE CASTLE OF THE POOR

Venant de très bas, de très loin,
nous arrivons au-delà.

Une longue chaîne d'amants
Sortit de la prison dont on prend l'habitude

Sur leur amour ils avaient tous juré
D'aller ensemble en se tenant la main
Ils étaient décidés à ne jamais céder
Un seul maillon de leur fraternité

La misère rampait encore sur les murs
La mort osait encore se montrer
Il n'y avait encore aucune loi parfaite
Aucun lien admirable

S'aimer était profane
S'unir était suspect

Ils voulaient s'enivrer d'eux-mêmes
Leurs yeux voulaient faire leur miel
Leur cœur voulait couver le ciel
Ils aimaient l'eau par les chaleurs
Ils étaient nés pour adorer le feu l'hiver

Ils avaient trop longtemps vécu contradictoires
Dans le chaos de l'esclavage
Rongeant leur frein lourds de fatigue et de méfaits
Ils se heurtaient entre eux étouffant les plus faibles

Quand ils criaient au secours
Ils se croyaient punissables ou fous
Leur drame était le repoussoir
De la félicité des maîtres

Que de baisers désespérés les menottes aux lèvres
Sous le soleil fécond que de retours à rien
Que de vaincus par le trop-plein de leur candeur
Empoignant un poignard pour prouver leur vertu

We had come from very far away and
arrived on the other side of the valley.

A long trail of lovers
Came out of the prison it becomes a matter of habit

On their love they had all sworn
To stay together holding hands
They had resolved never to surrender
A single link of their brotherhood

Distress still crept up the walls
Death still dared to be seen
There were still no ideal rules
No admirable vows

Loving one another was profane
Joining together was suspect

They wanted the wine of being together
Their eyes sought what could be turned to gain
Their hearts to gaze intently at the sky
They loved water in the great heat
They were born to worship fire in winter

Too long they had lived in the passion of conflict
In the confusion of slavery
Fought shy were burdened with fatigue and doing wrong
They jostled each other smothered the weakest

When they cried for help
They thought they were guilty or mad
Their tragedy was the setting scene
Of the joy of exploiters

What kisses of despair lips being shackled
Under the teeming sun what efforts come to nothing
What of those overcome by their innocence overflowing
Seizing a dagger to prove their worth

Ils étaient couronnés de leurs nerfs détraqués
On entendait hurler merci

Merci pour la faim et la soif
Merci pour le désastre et pour la mort bénie
Merci pour l'injustice
Mais qu'en attendez-vous et l'écho répondait

Nous nous délecterons de la monotonie
Nous nous embellirons de vêtements de deuil
Nous allons vivre un jour de plus
Nous les rapaces nous les rongeurs de ténèbres
Notre aveugle appétit s'exalte dans la boue
On ne verra le ciel que sur notre tombeau

Il y avait bien loin de ce Château des pauvres
Noir de crasse et de sang
Aux révoltes prévues aux récoltes possibles

Mais l'amour a toujours des marges si sensibles
Que les forces d'espoir s'y sont réfugiées
Pour mieux se libérer

Je t'aime je t'adore toi
Par-dessus la ligne des toits
Aux confins des vallées fertiles
Au seuil des rires et des îles
Où nul ne se noie ni ne brûle
Dans la foule future où nul
Ne peut éteindre son plaisir
La nuit protège le désir

L'horizon s'offre à la sagesse
Le cœur aux jeux de la jeunesse
Tout monte rien ne se retire

Their shattered nerves made fools of fools
We heard shouts of thank you

Thank you for hunger and thirst
Thank you for disaster and for blessed death
Thank you for injustice
But what do you want from this and the echo answered

We shall take delight in boredom
Adorn ourselves in the garments of mourning
We are going to live for one day more
We the birds of prey we the rats in the dark
Our senseless appetites will wallow in the mud
The sky you will see only over our graves

It was very far from this Castle of the Poor
Dark with dirt and blood
To the rebellions and harvests we could foresee

But love has always compassion enough
For the forces of hope to shelter there
The better to break free

I love you I worship you
Beyond the line of rooftops
To the edge of fertile valleys
To the gates of laughter and to islands
Where none shall drown or be consumed
In the crowd we shall know where no one
Can conceal his pleasure
Night protects desire

The horizon unfolds before wisdom
The heart before the eyes of youth
Everything rises nothing recedes

L'univers de fleurs violentes
Protège l'herbe la plus tendre
Je peux t'enclore entre mes bras
Pour me délivrer du passé
Je peux être agité tranquille
Sans rien déranger de ton rêve
Tu me veux simplement heureux
Et nous serons la porte ouverte
À la rosée au grand soleil
Et je t'entraîne dans ma fièvre
Jusqu'au jour le plus généreux

Il n'y a pas glaces qui tiennent
Devant la foudre et l'incendie
Devant les épis enflammés
D'un vrai baiser qui dit je t'aime
Graine absorbée par le sillon
Il n'y aura pas de problèmes
Minuscules si nous voyons
Ensemble l'aube à l'horizon
Comme un tremplin pour dépasser
Tout ce que nous avons été
Quand le crépuscule régnait

Toi la plus désespérée
Des esclaves dénuées
Toi qui venais de jamais
Sur une route déserte
Moi qui venais de très loin
Par mille sentiers croisés
Où l'homme ignore son bien
Innocent je t'ai fait boire
L'eau pure du miroir
Où je m'étais perdu
Minute par minute

Ce fut à qui donna
À l'autre l'illusion
D'avoir un peu vécu
Et de vouloir durer
Ainsi nous demeurâmes
Dans le Château des pauvres

A world of flushed flowers
Shields the sweetest grass
I can clasp you in my arms
To free myself from the past
I can be excited or at peace
Without disturbing what is in your dream
You simply wish me happiness
And we shall be the door that opens
To the early dew and the height of the sun
And I carry you away in my fever
As far as the kindest day of all

There is no ice that lasts
Against the lightning strike and fire
Against the bursting spikes of flowers
Of a kiss that says I love you
A seed that lies buried in the furrow's length
There will be no problems to worry us
If together we see
Day breaking over the distant sky
Like a place to leap and go beyond
All that we were
When dusk descended

You the most despairing
Of slaves in utter want
You who never came
Along an abandoned road
I who came from very far
Over a thousand paths that crossed
Where man knew nothing of his worth
Innocent I made you drink
The mirror's pure water
When I was losing my way
Minute by minute

One of us might give
To the other the illusion
Of knowing something of life
And of wishing to endure
So we stayed
In the Castle of the Poor

Au loin le paysage
S'aggravait d'inconnu
Et notre but notre salut
Se couvrait de nuages
Comme au jour du déluge

Château des pauvres les pauvres
Dormaient séparés d'eux-mêmes
Et vieillissaient solitaires
Dans un abîme de peines
Pauvreté les menait haut
Un peu plus haut que des bêtes
Ils pourrissaient leur château
La mousse mangeait la pierre
Et la lie dévastait l'eau
Le froid consumait les pauvres
La croix cachait le soleil

Ce n'était que sur leur fatigue
Sur leur sommeil que l'on comptait
Autour du Château des pauvres
Autour de toutes les victimes
Autour des ventres découverts
Pour enfanter et succomber
Et l'on disait donner la vie
C'est donner la mort à foison
Et l'on disait la poésie
Pour obnubiler la raison
Pour rendre aimable la prison

Pauvres dans le Château des pauvres
Nous fûmes deux et des millions
À caresser un très vieux songe
Il végétait plus bas que terre
Qu'il monte jusqu'à nos genoux
Et nous aurions été sauvés
Notre vie nous la concevions
Sans menaces et sans œillères
Nous pouvions adoucir les brutes
Et rayonnants nous alléger
Du fardeau même de la lutte

In the distance the landscape
Crumbled why we did not know
And our purpose and salvation
Were blanketed with clouds
As on a day of pouring rain

In the Castle of the Poor the poor
Slept separately from one another
Grew old alone
In a pitfall of distress
Poverty drove them hard
Harder than beasts are driven
They let their castle rot
The moss ate away the stone
And the lees poisoned the water
The cold wore the poor to a shadow
The cross hid the sun

It was only on their weariness
Only on their sleep that we depended
All around the Castle of the Poor
Among all the victims
Among the maws laid bare
To beget and to yield
And we said the gift of life
Was the gift of death in plenty
And we said that poetry
Would becloud the reason
For making of prison a pleasant place

Poor in the Castle of the Poor
We were two people and millions
Believing in a very old dream
It lay in silence out of sight
Had it risen there before us
We would have been saved
Our lives we conceived
Without threats or scales before our eyes
We could pacify the beasts
And wrapped in smiles made light for us
The very burden of the fight

Les aveugles nous contemplent
Les pires sourds nous entendent
Ils parviennent à sourire
Il ne nous en faut pas plus
Pour tamiser l'épouvante
De subsister sans défense
Il ne nous en faut pas plus
Pour nous épouser sans crainte
Nous nous voyons nous entendons
Comme si nous donnions à tous
Le pouvoir d'être sans contrainte

Si notre amour est ce qu'il est
C'est qu'il a franchi ses limites
Il voulait passer sous la haie
Comme un serpent et gagner l'air
Comme un oiseau et gagner l'onde
Comme un poisson gagner le temps
Gagner la vie contre la mort
Et perpétuer l'univers

Tu m'as murmuré perfection
Moi je t'ai soufflé harmonie
Quand nous nous sommes embrassés
Un grand silence s'est levé
Notre nudité délirante
Nous a fait soudain tout comprendre
Quoi qu'il arrive nous rêvons
Quoi qu'il arrive nous vivrons

Tu tends ton front comme une route
Où rien ne me fait trébucher
Le soleil y fond goutte à goutte
Pas à pas j'y reprends des forces
De nouvelles raisons d'aimer
Et le monde sous son écorce
M'offre sa sève conjuguée
Au long ruisseau de nos baisers

The blind observe us
The deafest hear us
They manage to smile
We need no more
To drain the horror
Of existence that has no defence
We need no more
To come together without fear
We see and understand each other
As though we were giving to everyone
The power to exist without restraint

If our love is the love it is
The reason is it knew no bounds
It sought to slide under the hedge
To seek the air like a serpent
To seek the wave like a bird
And to seek time like a fish
For life to triumph over death
For the world to be ever flowing

You murmured to me about perfection
I whispered to you about harmony
When we kissed
A great silence reigned
Our rapturous nakedness
At once made everything understood
Whatever happens we dream
Whatever happens we shall live

You look before you and like a road
Where nothing makes me falter
The sun melts drop by drop
Step by step I recover strength
Find new reasons for loving
And the world from under its shell
Gives me its sap that runs
Into the long stream of our kisses

Quoi qu'il arrive nous vivrons
Et du fond du Château des pauvres
Où nous avons tant de semblables
Tant de complices tant d'amis
Monte la voile du courage
Hissons-la sans hésiter
Demain nous saurons pourquoi
Quand nous aurons triomphé

Une longue chaîne d'amants
Sortit de la prison dont on prend l'habitude

La dose d'injustice et la dose de honte
Sont vraiment trop amères

Il ne faut pas de tout pour faire un monde il faut
Du bonheur et rien d'autre

Pour être heureux il faut simplement y voir clair
Et lutter sans défaut

Nos ennemis sont fous débiles maladroits
Il faut en profiter

N'attendons pas un seul instant levons la tête
Prenons d'assaut la terre

Nous le savons elle est à nous submergeons-la
Nous sommes invincibles

Une longue chaîne d'amants
Sortit de la prison dont on prend l'habitude

Au printemps ils se fortifièrent
L'été leur fut un vêtement un aliment
L'hiver ils crurent au cristal aux sommets bleus
La lumière baigna leurs yeux
De son alcool de sa jeunesse permanente

Ô ma maîtresse Dominique ma compagne
Comme la flamme qui s'attaque au mur sans paille
Nous avons manqué de patience
Nous en sommes récompensés

Whatever happens we shall live
And from inside the Castle of the Poor
Where we have so many of our kind
So many companions so many friends
Raise high the banner of courage
Let us hoist it no need to hesitate
Tomorrow we shall know why
When we have triumphed

A long trail of lovers
Came out of the prison it becomes a matter of habit

The potion of injustice and the potion of shame
Are really too bitter

No need to have everything to make a world
You need happiness and nothing else

To be happy we just need to see clearly
Struggle and never falter

Our enemies are clumsy mad and weak
We must seize our chance

Let us not wait a single moment lift up our heads
Let us take the earth by storm

This we know it is ours we shall bury it
We cannot be vanquished

A long trail of lovers
Came out of the prison it becomes a matter of habit

In the spring they grew stronger
Summer to them was food and clothing
In winter they crystal gazed at the blue heights
The light bathed their eyes
With the alcohol of its lasting youth

O mistress Dominique O my companion
Like the flame attacking a strawless wall
We have lacked patience
We are rewarded now

Tu veux la vie à l'infini moi la naissance
Tu veux le fleuve moi la source
Nul brouillard ne nous a voilés
Et simplement dans la clarté je te retrouve

Vois les ruines déjà du Château qu'on oublie
Il n'avait pas d'architecture définie
Il n'avait pas de toit
Il n'avait pas d'armure
Agonies et défaites y resplendissaient
La naissance y était obscure

Vois l'ombre transparente du Château des pauvres
Qui fut notre berceau notre vieille misère
Rions à travers elle
Rions du beau temps fixe qui nous met au monde

Il s'est fait un climat sur terre plus subtil
Que la montée du jour fertile
C'est le climat de nos amours
Et nous en jouissons car nous le comprenons

Il est la vérité sa clarté nous inonde

Nous étendons la fleur de la vie ses couleurs
Le meilleur de nous-mêmes
Par-delà toute nuit
Notre cœur nous conduit
Notre tendresse unit les heures

Ce matin un oiseau chante
Ce soir une femme espère
L'oiseau chante pour demain
La femme nous reproduit

Le vieux mensonge est absorbé
Par les plus drus rochers par la plus grasse glèbe
Par la vague par l'herbe
Les pièges sont rouillés

You seek an infinite life I the moment of birth
You seek the river I the source
No mists have veiled our eyes
And so I find you in the shining light

Look at the ruins already forgotten
No particular design
No roof
No defences
Death and defeat were plain to see
Origin was a mystery

See through the lucent shadows of the Castle of the Poor
That was our cradle our old distress
Let us laugh our way through the shadows
Laugh at the time set fair that brings us here

There spreads abroad a sensation more subtle
Than the rise of the lush day
A sensation made of the things we love
And we rejoice because we understand

It is the truth its splendour overwhelms us

We scatter the bloom of life
Its colours the proof of us
Beyond all darkness
Our hearts guide us
Our tenderness joins the hours together

This morning a bird sings
This evening a woman hopes
The bird sings for tomorrow
The woman multiplies

The old falsehood is contained
By the hardest rock and the richest soil
By wave by grass
The traps have rusted

Sur la ligne droite qui mène
La cascade à son point de chute
Et sur la longue inclinaison
Qui torture le cours du fleuve
Se fixent mille points d'aplomb
Où la vue et la vie s'émeuvent
Éblouies ou se reposant

Fleuve et cascade du présent
Comme un seul battement de cœur
Pour l'unique réseau du sang
L'eau se mêle à l'espoir visible
Je vois une vallée peuplée
Des grands gardiens de l'ordre intime
L'exaltation jointe à la paix

L'homme courbé qui se redresse
Qui se délasse et crie victoire
Vers son prochain vers l'infini
Le jour souple qui se détend
Moulant la terre comme un gant
L'étincelle devient diamant
La vague enflammée un étang

Tout se retourne la moisson
Devient le grain du blé crispé
La fleur se retrouve bouton
Le désir et l'enfant s'abreuvent
De même chair de même lait
Et la nuit met sous les paupières
De l'homme et de l'eau la même ombre

La vie au cours du temps la vie
Le réel et l'imaginaire
Sont ses deux mains et ses deux yeux
Ma table pèse mon poème
Mon écriture l'articule
L'image l'offre à tout venant
Chacun s'y trouve ressemblant

On the straight line that leads
The waterfall to its drop
And on the long incline
That bends the course of the river
So many splashes of water will settle
Where vision and life will stir one another
Dazzled or come to rest

Waterfall and river of the here and now
Like the single beat of a heart
For the flow of the blood that reigns
Water blends with the hope I see
I see a valley inhabited
By the great guardians of inmost law
Rapture added to peace

The stooping man who stands upright again
Refreshed and shouting victory
To his neighbour and to infinity
The lengthening day unfolding
Fitting the earth like a glove
The spark becomes a diamond
The restless wave a pond

Everything is reversed the harvest
Becomes the shrivelled corn
The flower returns to bud again
Desire and the child drink their fill
From the same flesh the same milk
And night casts the same shadows
Over the waters and the eyes of men

Life in the flow of time
The real and the imaginary
Are its two hands and two eyes
My table ponders over my poem
My writing finds the words
The image is displayed to any comer
Each finds his likeness there

Le réel c'est la bonne part
L'imaginaire c'est l'espoir
Confus qui m'a mené vers toi
À travers tant de bons refus
À travers tant de rages froides
Tant de puériles aventures
D'enthousiasmes de déceptions

Souviens-toi du Château des pauvres
De ces haillons que nous traînions
Et vrai nous croyions pavoiser
Nous reflétions un monde idiot
Riions quand il fallait pleurer
Voyions en rose la vie rouge
Absolvions ce qui nous ruinait

Dis-toi que je parle pour toi
Plus que pour moi puisque je t'aime
Et que tu te souviens pour moi
De mon passé par mes poèmes
Comment pourrais-tu m'en vouloir
Ne comptons jamais sur hier
Tout l'ancien temps n'est que chimères

De même que je t'aime enfant
Et jeune fille il faut m'aimer
Comme un homme et comme un amant
Dans ton univers nouveau-né
Nous avions tous deux les mains vides
Quand nous nous sommes abordés
Et nous nous sommes pensés libres

Il ne fallait rien renoncer
Que le mal de la solitude
Il ne fallait rien abdiquer
Que l'orgueil vain d'avoir été
En dépit de la servitude
Ô disais-tu mon cœur existe
Mon cœur bat en dépit de tout

The real is the solid part
The imaginary the shadowy hope
That guided my steps towards you
Through so much good denied
Through so much silent anger
So much boyish adventuring
Enthusiasm and blighted hope

Remember the Castle of the Poor
Those rags we used to drag behind us
We really believed we could celebrate
We the children of a senseless world
Laughed when we should have cried
Saw raw life in pretty colours
Were ready to forgive what would destroy

Say that I speak for you
More than for myself because I love you
And that about me you remember
My past times through my poems
How could you wish me angered with myself
Let us never depend on yesterday
All the past is only idle fancy

Just as I love you child
And girl I must be loved
As a man and as a lover
In your world so very new
We were empty-handed both of us
When we came to know each other
And thought that we were free

We did not need to renounce
Anything but the pain of loneliness
We did not need to yield
Anything but the pride we both once had
In spite of servitude
O did you say this is my heart
My heart is beating in spite of everything

Je ne mens jamais ni ne doute
Je t'aime comme on vient au monde
Comme le ciel éclate et règne
Je suis la lettre initiale
Des mots que tu cherchas toujours
La majuscule l'idéale
Qui te commande de m'aimer

Dans le Château des pauvres je n'ai pu t'offrir
Que de dire ton cœur comme je dis mon cœur
Sans ombre de douleur sans ombre de racines
En enfant frère des enfants qui renaîtront
Toujours pour confirmer notre amour et l'amour

Le long effort des hommes vers leur cohésion
Cette chaîne qui sort de la géhenne ancienne
Est soudée à l'or pur au feu de la franchise
Elle respire elle voit clair et ses maillons
Sont tous des yeux ouverts que l'espoir égalise

La vérité fait notre joie écoute-moi
Je n'ai plus rien à te cacher tu dois me voir
Tel que je suis plus faible et plus fort que les autres
Plus fort tenant ta main plus faible pour les autres
Mais j'avoue et c'est là la raison de me croire

J'avoue je viens de loin et j'en reste éprouvé
Il y a des moments où je renonce à tout
Sans raisons simplement parce que la fatigue
M'entraîne jusqu'au fond des brumes du passé
Et mon soleil se cache et mon ombre s'étend

Vois-tu je ne suis pas tout à fait innocent
Et malgré moi malgré colères et refus
Je représente un monde accablant corrompu
L'eau de mes jours n'a pas toujours été changée
Je n'ai pas toujours pu me soustraire à la vase

Mes mains et ma pensée ont été obligées
Trop souvent de se refermer sur le hasard
Je me suis trop souvent laissé aller et vivre
Comme un miroir éteint faute de recevoir
Suffisamment d'images et de passions
Pour accroître le poids de ma réflexion

I never deceive nor do I doubt
I love you as one is born
As the heavens shine and reign
I am the first letter
Of the words you sought always
The capital letter the perfect letter
Bidding you to love me

In the Castle of the Poor all I could do
Was to tell of your heart as I told of mine
Unshadowed of distress unshadowed of beginnings
As child and brother of children to be born again
Always to seal our love and love

The long march of men to their unity
This chain from out of a bygone hell
Is welded in pure gold in the fire of freedom
It breathes sees the way ahead and its links
Are all the open eyes that hope has made the same

Truth makes our joy listen to me
I have no more to hide you must see me
As I am weaker and stronger than other men
Stronger holding your hand weaker with others
This I confess and there is the reason for believing me

I confess I come from far still tried by distance
Times when I am casting everything aside
Without a reason only because my weariness
Drags me back to the far mists of the past
And my sun hides and my shadow lengthens

I am not you see entirely free of blame
In spite of myself in spite of temper and denial
I belong to a world corrupt and overpowering
The run of my days knew little change of course
I could not always break free from the mire

Too often were my thoughts and hands
Compelled to clench and close on chance
Too often it was letting go and letting live
As a mirror darkens when it lacks
Enough of light and passion
To define the weight of my own reflection

Il me fallait rêver sans ordre et sans logique
Sans savoir sans mémoire pour ne pas vieillir
Mais ce que j'ai souffert de ne pouvoir déduire
L'avenir de mon cœur fugitif dis-le toi
Toi qui sais comment j'ai tenté de m'associer
À l'espoir harmonieux d'un bonheur assuré

Dis-le toi la raison la plus belle à mes yeux
Ma quotidienne bien-aimée ma bien-aimante
Faut-il que je ressente ou faut-il que j'invente
Le moment du printemps le cloître de l'été
Pour me sentir capable de te rendre heureuse
Au cœur fou de la foule et seule à mes côtés

Nul de nous deux n'a peur du lendemain dis-tu
Notre cœur est gonflé de graines éclatées
Et nous saurons manger le fruit de la vertu
Sa neige se dissipe en lumières sucrées
Nous le reproduirons comme il nous a conçus
Chacun sur un versant du jour vers le sommet

Oui c'est pour aujourd'hui que je t'aime ma belle
Le présent pèse sur nous deux et nous soulève
Mieux que le ciel soulève un oiseau vent debout
C'est aujourd'hui qu'est née la joie et je marie
La courbe de la vague à l'aile d'un sourire
C'est aujourd'hui que le présent est éternel

Je n'ai aucune idée de ce que tu mérites
Sauf d'être aimée et bien aimée au fond des âges
Ma limite et mon infini dans ce minuit
Qui nous a confondus pour la vie à jamais
En nous abandonnant nous étions davantage

Ce minuit-là nous fûmes les enfants d'hier
Sortant de leur enfance en se tenant la main
Nous nous étions trouvés retrouvés reconnus
Et le matin bonjour dîmes-nous à la vie
À notre vie ancienne et future et commune

À tout ce que le temps nous infuse de force.

I had to dream thoughtless and with abandon
Unknowing no memories in order not to age
But how I suffered for not reasoning out
The future of my fugitive heart remember
You who know how I tried to share
The unstrained hope of happiness made sure

Remember the most beautiful reason in my eyes
My beloved of every day my loving one
Must I feel must I invent
The breath of spring the hush of summer
To feel within me I can make you happy
In the rapture of the crowd or alone at my side

You say that neither of us fears the morrow
Our hearts are filled with ripening seeds
And we shall know how to eat the fruit of virtue
Its whiteness vanishes in sweetened light
We shall recreate it as it had conceived us both
Each on the slope of the day to the mountain top

Yes it is today that I love you my beautiful one
The present bears upon us both and lifts us
Better than sky lifts a bird upwind
It is today that joy is born and I join
The curve of the wave to the wing of a smile
It is today that the present is eternal

I cannot tell what you deserve
Save to be loved and fondly loved to the far away years
Far to my boundlessness upon this strike of twelve
That joined our hands together once for all
We were the richer giving all to each and each

That midnight we were yesterday's children
Leaving behind their childhood holding hands
We were found discovered recognised
And in the morning we said good-day to life
To our past and future lives and to our life together

To everything that time with strength endows.

Bloodaxe Contemporary French Poets

Series Editors: Timothy Mathews & Michael Worton

FRENCH-ENGLISH BILINGUAL EDITIONS

1: **Yves Bonnefoy:** *On the Motion and Immobility of Douve /*
   Du mouvement et de l'immobilité de Douve
   Trans. Galway Kinnell. Introduction: Timothy Mathews. £12
2: **René Char:** *The Dawn Breakers / Les Matinaux*
   Trans. & intr. Michael Worton. £12
3: **Henri Michaux:** *Spaced, Displaced / Déplacements Dégagements*
   Trans. David & Helen Constantine. Introduction: Peter Broome. £12
4: **Aimé Césaire:** *Notebook of a Return to My Native Land /*
   Cahier d'un retour au pays natal
   Trans. & intr. Mireille Rosello (with Annie Pritchard). £12
5: **Philippe Jaccottet:** *Under Clouded Skies / Beauregard*
   Pensées sous les nuages / Beauregard
   Trans. David Constantine & Mark Treharne.
   Introduction: Mark Treharne. £12
6: **Paul Éluard:** *Unbroken Poetry II / Poésie ininterrompue II*
   Trans. Gilbert Bowen. Introduction: Jill Lewis. £12
7: **André Frénaud:** *Rome the Sorceress / La Sorcière de Rome*
   Trans. Keith Bosley. Introduction: Peter Broome. £8.95
8: **Gérard Macé:** *Wood Asleep / Bois dormant*
   Trans. David Kelley. Introduction: Jean-Pierre Richard. £8.95
9: **Guillevic:** *Carnac*
   Trans. John Montague. Introduction: Stephen Romer. £12
10: **Salah Stétié:** *Cold Water Shielded: Selected Poems*
    Trans. & intr. Michael Bishop. £9.95

'Bloodaxe's Contemporary French Poets series could not have arrived at a more opportune time, and I cannot remember any translation initiative in the past thirty years that has been more ambitious or more coherently planned in its attempt to bring French poetry across the Channel and the Atlantic. Under the editorship of Timothy Mathews and Michael Worton, the series has a clear format and an even clearer sense of mission' – MALCOLM BOWIE, *TLS*